Cameos
of
Christmas

Compiled and Edited
by
Joan Revill

Yes, they can make, who fail to find
Short leisure even in busiest days,
Moments, to cast a look behind,
And profit by those kindly rays
That through the clouds do sometimes steal,
And all the far-off past reveal.

William Wordsworth
Sonnets to the River Duddon

First Published in Great Britain in 2003 by Barny Books
Text © Joan Revill
All rights reserved
Design © TUCANN*design&print*

ISBN N° 1 903172 40 3

Produced by: TUCANN*design&print*, 19 High Street, Heighington Lincoln LN4 1RG
Tel & Fax: 01522 790009
www.tucann.co.uk

Contents

Acknowledgements

For permission to reprint extracts from copyright material, the editor gratefully acknowledges the following:

"Farmer's Boy" by John R. Allan reproduced by permission of Ardo Publishing Company.

"The Fir-Tree" by Hans Christian Andersen translated by W. L. Kingsland from *Fairy Tales from Hans Andersen* (OUP. 1999) reproduced by permission of Oxford University Press.

"Goodwill to Men: Give Us Your Money" by Pam Ayres from "The Works: Selected Poems" by Pam Ayres reproduced with the permission of BBC Worldwide Limited. Copyright © Pam Ayres 1992.

"A Remaining Christmas" by Hilaire Belloc published by the Stanbrook Abbey Press.

"Christmas" by John Betjeman from "Collected Poems" published by John Murray (Publishers) Ltd.

"Testament of Friendship" by Vera Brittain by permission of Mark Bosbridge and Rebecca Williams, her literary executors.

"Over the Bridge" by Richard Church published by Heinemann.

"More William" by Richmal Crompton published by Macmillan Children's Books, London, U.K.

"The Christmas Tree" by C. Day Lewis: The Complete Poems by C. Day Lewis published by Sinclair-Stevenson (1992), copyright © 1992 in this edition, and the Estate of C. Day Lewis. Used by permission of The Random House Group Ltd.

"The Dean's Watch", "Island Magic", "The Christmas Book", "Towers in the Mist"and "TheHerb of Grace" by Elizabeth Goudge published by David Higham Associates.

"Let Sleeping Vets Lie" by James Herriot published by Michael Joseph.

"Mr Ives' Christmas" by Oscar Hijuelos published by Bloomsbury.

"The Magic Apple Tree" by Susan Hill published by Penguin Books. Copyright © 1982 by Susan Hill.

"The Very Dead of Winter" by Mary Hocking published by Chatto & Windus. Used by permission of The Random House Group Ltd.

Preface

We all love to see the happy Victorian scenes which appear on our Christmas cards – the jolly family gathered around the laden festive board; the horse-drawn stagecoach bowling along in a snowy, country landscape; the lady in the crinoline dress, poke bonnet and fur muff, accompanied by the gentleman in frock-coat and top hat, looking in at the small-paned, bow-fronted shop window; the skating party. These images of happy family gatherings conjure up a cosy glow not only on the cards but in our hearts. They allow us to escape for a while from the hustle and bustle of our everyday lives. Distance lends enchantment to the view and we look back with nostalgia to a period which, superficially at least, seems to have been a simpler, homelier time.

But this nostalgia applies not only to a bygone era, it also extends to our own personal lives. For at Christmas we delve into our store of childhood memories and look back to a time when we were young and innocent, when life for us was carefree and Christmas seemed full of magic.

I have tried to create this feeling not with pictures painted by the artist's brush, but with words from the writer's pen. This selection of descriptive passages, which evoke this "cosy glow", has been arranged in chronological order of content, starting with preparations and finishing with a brief look back over the festive season, then to the future, so as to create a gradual build-up of expectation as Christmas approaches and fulfilment as it progresses.

The time and the place may vary but the essence of Christmas remains the same. Long may it remain so.

1
What is Christmas?

At Christmas play and make good cheer,
For Christmas comes but once a year.
At Christmas be merry and thankful withal
And feast thy poor neighbour, the great with the small.

THOMAS TUSSER
The Farmers' Daily Diet 1557
(Five Hundred Points of Good Husbandry)

Close the shutters, and draw the curtains together, and pile fresh wood upon the hearth! Let us have, for once, an innocent *auto de fe*. Let the hoarded corks be brought forth, and branches of crackling laurel. Place the wine and fruit and the hot chestnuts upon the table. And now, good folks and children, bring your chairs round to the blazing fire. Put some of those rosy apples upon your plates. We'll drink one glass of bright sherry "To our absent friends" and then talk a little about Christmas.

It is the happiest time of the year. It is the season of mirth and cold weather. It is the time when Christmas-boxes and jokes are given; when mistletoe, and red-berried laurel, and soups, and sliding, and school-boys, prevail; when the country is illuminated by fires and bright faces; and the town is radiant with laughing children...

Oh! merry piping time of Christmas! Never let us permit thee to degenerate into distant courtesies and formal salutations. But let us shake our friends and familiars by the hand, as our fathers and their fathers did. Let them all come around us, and let us count how many the year has added to our circle.

CHARLES LAMB
A Few Words on Christmas 1829
(Sketches and Essays)

Of all the old festivals, however, that of Christmas awakens the strongest and most heartfelt associations. There is a tone of solemn and sacred feeling that blends with our conviviality, and lifts the spirit to a state of hallowed and elevated enjoyment. The services of the church about this season are extremely tender and inspiring. They dwell on the beautiful story of the origin of our faith, and the pastoral scenes that accompanied its announcement. They gradually increase in fervour and pathos during the season of Advent, until they break forth in full jubilee on the morning that brought peace and good will to men. I do not know a grander effect of music on the moral feelings, than to hear the full choir and the pealing organ performing a Christmas anthem in a cathedral, and filling every part of the vast pile with triumphant harmony.

It is a beautiful arrangement, also, derived from days of yore, that this festival, which commemorates the announcement of the religion of peace and love, has been made the season for gathering together of family connexions, and drawing closer again those bands of kindred hearts, which the cares and pleasures and sorrows of the world are continually operating to cast loose; of calling back the children of a family, who have launched forth in life, and wandered widely asunder, once more to assemble about the paternal hearth, that rallying place of the affections, there to grow young and loving again among the endearing mementos of childhood.

The English, from the great prevalence of rural habits throughout every class of society, have always been fond of those festivals and holydays which agreeably interrupt the stillness of country life; and they were, in former days, particularly observant of the religious and social rites of Christmas. It is inspiring to read even the dry details which some antiquaries have given of the quaint humours, the burlesque pageants, the complete abandonment to mirth and good fellowship, with which this festival was celebrated. It seemed to throw open every door, and unlock every heart. It brought the peasant and the peer together, and blended all ranks in one warm generous flow of joy and kindness. The old halls of castles and manor houses resounded with the harp and the Christmas carol, and their ample boards groaned under the weight of hospitality. Even the poorest cottage welcomed the festive season with green decorations of bay and holly - the cheerful fire glanced its rays through the lattice, inviting the passenger to raise the latch, and join the gossip knot huddled round the hearth, beguiling the long evening with legendary jokes, and oft told Christmas tales.

One of the least pleasing effects of modern refinement is the havoc it has made among the hearty old holyday customs. Many of the games and ceremonials of Christmas have entirely disappeared. The traditionary customs of golden hearted antiquity, its feudal hospitalities, and lordly wassailings, have passed away with the baronial castles and stately manor houses in which they were celebrated. They comported with the shadowy hall, the great oaken gallery, and the tapestried parlour, but were unfitted to the light showy saloons and gay drawing rooms of the modern villa.

Shorn, however, as it is, of its ancient and festive honours, Christmas is still a period of delightful excitement in England. It is gratifying to see that home feeling completely aroused which holds so powerful a place in every English bosom. The preparations making on every side for the social board that is again to unite friends and kindred - the presents of good cheer passing and repassing, those tokens of regard and quickeners of kind feelings - the evergreens distributed about houses and churches, emblems of peace and gladness – all these have the most pleasing effect in producing fond associations, and kindling benevolent sympathies. Even the sound of the Waits, rude as may be their minstrelsy, breaks upon the midwatches of a winter night with the effect of perfect harmony. As I have been awakened by them in that still and solemn hour "when deep sleep falleth upon man," I have listened with hushed delight, and connecting them with the sacred and joyous occasion, have almost fancied them into another celestial choir, announcing peace and good will to mankind.

Amidst the general call to happiness, the bustle of the spirits, and stir of the affections, which prevail at this period, what bosom can remain insensible? It is, indeed, the season of regenerated feeling – the season for kindling not merely the fire of hospitality in the hall, but the genial flame of charity in the heart.

WASHINGTON IRVING
Sketch Book 1820

Christmas time! That man must be a misanthrope indeed, in whose breast something like a jovial feeling is not roused - in whose mind some pleasant associations are not awakened - by the recurrence of Christmas. There are people who will tell you that Christmas is not to them what it used to be; that each succeeding Christmas has found some cherished hope, or happy prospect, of the year before, dimmed or passed away; that the present only serves to remind them of reduced circumstances and straitened incomes - of the feasts they once bestowed on hollow friends, and of the cold looks that meet them now, in adversity and misfortune. Never heed such dismal reminiscences. There are few men who have lived long enough in the world, who cannot call up such thoughts any day in the year. Then do not select the merriest of the three hundred and sixty-five for your doleful recollections, but draw your chair nearer the blazing fire – fill the glass and send round the song – and if your room be smaller than it was a dozen years ago, or if your glass be filled with reeking punch, instead of sparkling wine, put a good face on the matter, and empty it off-hand, and fill another, and troll off the old ditty you used to sing, and thank God it's no worse. Look on the merry faces of your children as they sit around the fire. Reflect upon your present blessings – of which every man has many – not on your past misfortunes, of which all men have some. Fill your glass again with a merry face and contented heart. Our life on it, but your Christmas shall be merry and your new year a happy one!

Who can be insensible to the outpourings of good feeling, and the honest interchange of affectionate attachment which abound at this season of the year? A Christmas family party! We know nothing in nature more delightful! There seems a magic in the very name of Christmas. Petty jealousies and discords are forgotten; social feelings are awakened, in bosoms to which they have long been strangers; father and son, or brother and sister, who have met and passed with averted gaze, or a look of cold recognition, for months before, proffer and return the cordial embrace, and bury their past animosities in their present happiness. Kindly hearts that have yearned towards each other but have been withheld by false notions of pride and self-dignity, are again reunited, and all is kindness and benevolence! Would that Christmas lasted the whole year through (as it ought), and that the prejudices and passions which deform our better nature, were never called into action among those to whom they should ever be strangers!

CHARLES DICKENS
Sketches by Boz 1834

Christmas was close at hand, in all his bluff and hearty honesty; it was the season of hospitality, merriment, and open-heartedness; the old year was preparing, like an ancient philosopher, to call his friends around him, and amidst the sound of feasting and revelry to pass gently and calmly away. Gay and merry was the time, and gay and merry were the numerous hearts that were gladdened by its coming.

And numerous indeed are the hearts to which Christmas brings a brief season of happiness and enjoyment. How many families, whose members have been dispersed and scattered far and wide, in the restless struggles of life, are then reunited, and meet once again in that happy state of companionship and mutual good-will, which is a source of such pure and unalloyed delight, and one so incompatible with the cares and sorrows of the world, that the religious belief of the most civilised nations, and the rude traditions of the roughest savages, alike number it among the first joys of a future condition of existence, provided for the blest and happy! How many old recollections, and how many dormant sympathies, does Christmas time awaken!

Happy, happy Christmas, that can win us back to the delusions of our childish days; that can recall to the old man the pleasures of his youth; that can transport the sailor and the traveller, thousands of miles away, back to his own fire-side and his quiet home!

CHARLES DICKENS
The Pickwick Papers 1837

I have always thought of Christmas time, when it comes round – apart from the veneration due to its sacred name and origin, if anything belonging to it can be apart from that – as a good time; a kind, forgiving, charitable, pleasant time; the only time I know of, in the long calendar of the year, when men and women seem by one consent to open their shut-up hearts freely, and to think of people below them as if they really were fellow-passengers to the grave, and not another race of creatures bound on other journeys. And therefore, I say, "God bless it!"

CHARLES DICKENS
A Christmas Carol 1843

One of the greatest pleasures Christmas brings is the assembling of members of families – the bringing together once more of all the old familiar faces around the household hearth. To see the venerable father and mother still occupying their old armchairs; to sit at the same place at the table which they formerly claimed as their own, beside the sister with whom they once kissed and quarrelled a dozen times a day, yet loved all the more after each childish squabble – these are the little home touches that send a silent thrill through the heart, and force tears into the eyes unawares.

Illustrated London News 1849

Time was, with most of us, when Christmas day, encircling all our limited world like a magic ring, left nothing out for us to miss or seek; bound together all our home enjoyments, affections, and hopes; grouped everything and every one around the Christmas fire; and made the little picture shining in our bright young eyes, complete.

As we grow older, let us be more thankful that the circle of our Christmas associations and of the lessons that they bring, expands! Let us welcome every one of them, and summon them to take their places by the Christmas hearth.

Welcome, old aspirations, glittering creatures of an ardent fancy, to your shelter underneath the holly! We know you, and have not outlived you yet. Welcome, old projects and old loves, however fleeting, to your nooks among the steadier lights that burn around us. Welcome, all that was ever real to our hearts; and for the earnestness that made you real, thanks to Heaven! Do we build no Christmas castles in the clouds now? Let our thoughts, fluttering like butterflies among these flowers of children, bear witness!

Welcome everything! Welcome alike, what has been, and what never was, and what we hope may be, to your shelter underneath the holly, to your places round the Christmas fire, where what is sits open-hearted! In yonder shadow, do we see obtruding furtively upon the blaze, an enemy's face? By Christmas Day we do forgive him! If the injury he has done us may admit of such companionship, let

14

him come here and take his place. If otherwise, unhappily, let him go hence, assured that we will never injure nor accuse him. On this day we shut out Nothing. On Christmas Day, we will shut out from our fireside, Nothing.

In town and village, there are doors and windows closed against the weather, there are flaming logs heaped high, there are joyful faces, there is healthy music of voices. Be all ungentleness and harm excluded from the temples of the household gods, but be those remembrances admitted with tender encouragement! They are of the time and all its comforting and peaceful reassurances.

CHARLES DICKENS
What Christmas is as we Grow Older 1851
(Christmas Stories)

On Christmas Day England gathers around the hearthstone and assembles in the family. The son separated by the cares of the world in the battle for life is reunited with his father, his mother and his sisters. But this grand opportunity of reuniting the love of families is in some danger of being lost to us. Our intense commercial life has brought with it something of a peripatetic existence to us all. Locomotion has changed the face of English society. A family that, forty years ago, would have been easily gathered together at an hour's notice, cannot now be assembled except at great inconvenience to every member, at great expense and with notice. The struggle for existence calls away boys from the roof of the parent into the crowded and busy city. The daughter too has left her mother's admonishing but tender eye. To such, a recurrence of Christmas is the only opportunity of joyful reunion. The youth living in the centre of a great city surrounded by temptation and companions ready to lead him astray, may be stayed in his course by a visit to his early home.

Morning Chronicle - Christmas Editorial 1860

It is fashion, I believe, to regard Christmas as a bore of rather a gross description, and as a time when you are invited to over-eat yourself, and pretend to be merry without just cause. As a matter of fact, it is one of the prettiest and most poetic institutions possible, if observed in the proper manner, and after having been more or less unpleasant to everybody for a whole year, it is a blessing to be forced on that one day to be amiable, and it is certainly delightful to be able to give presents without being haunted by the conviction that you are spoiling the recipient, and will suffer for it afterwards.

I cannot see that there is anything gross about our Christmas, and we were perfectly merry without any need to pretend, and for at least two days it brought us a little nearer together, and made us kind. Happiness is so wholesome.

ELIZABETH VON ARNIM
Elizabeth and her German Garden 1898

Is Christmas the smell of evergreen,
The jingle of bells on a sleigh;
Is Christmas the laughter of children,
The greeting of friends in the way?
Is Christmas the lighting of candles,
The hanging of wreaths on the door;
Is Christmas the welcome of loved ones?
Yes, Christmas is this and more.

For Christmas echoes from angels
Its message of peace and good will;
And Christmas tells of a manger
On a calm Judean hill,
Where shepherds bowed and worshipped
As God incarnate slept,
And it's only as we kneel with them
That our Christmas is truly kept.

VERNA S. TEEUWISSEN
Keeping Christmas 2002

2
Preparations

The bells of waiting Advent ring,
The Tortoise stove is lit again

And lamp-oil light across the night
Has caught the streaks of winter rain
In many a stained-glass window sheen

From Crimson Lake to Hooker's Green.

The holly in the windy hedge
And round the Manor House the yew
Will soon be stripped to deck the ledge,
The altar, font and arch and pew,
So that the villagers can say
"The church looks nice" on Christmas Day.

Provincial public houses blaze
And Corporation tramcars clang,
On lighted tenements I gaze
Where paper decorations hang,
And bunting in the red Town Hall
Says "Merry Christmas to you all."

And London shops on Christmas Eve
Are strung with silver bells and flowers
As hurrying clerks the city leave
To pigeon-haunted classic towers,
And marbled clouds go scudding by
The many-steepled London sky.

And girls in slacks remember Dad,
And oafish louts remember Mum,
And sleepless children's hearts are glad,
And Christmas-morning bells say "Come!"
Even to the shining ones who dwell
Safe in the Dorchester Hotel.

And is it true? And is it true,
This most tremendous tale of all,
Seen in a stained-glass window's hue,
A Baby in an ox's stall?
The Maker of the stars and sea
Become a Child on earth for me?

And is it true? For if it is,
No loving fingers tying strings
Around those tissued fripperies,
The sweet and silly Christmas things,
Bath salts and inexpensive scent
And hideous tie so kindly meant,

No love that in a family dwells,
No carolling in frosty air,
Nor all the steeple-shaking bells
Can with this single Truth compare -
That God was Man in Palestine
And lives to-day in Bread and Wine.

SIR JOHN BETJEMAN
Christmas
(A Few Late Chrysanthemums 1954)

A more amusing episode was that of the barrels of beer. At that time in that part of the country, brewers' travellers, known locally as "outriders", called for orders at farm-houses and superior cottages, as well as at inns. No experienced outrider visited farm labourers' cottages; but the time came when a beginner, full of youthful enthusiasm and burning to fill up his order book, had the brilliant idea of canvassing the hamlet for orders.

Wouldn't it be splendid, he asked the women, to have their own nine-gallon cask of good ale in for Christmas, and only have to go into the pantry and turn the tap to get a glass for their husband and friends. The ale cost far less by the barrel than when bought at the inn. It would be an economy in the long run, and how well it would look to bring out a jug of foaming ale from their own barrel for their friends. As to payment, they sent in their bills quarterly, so there would be plenty of time to save up.

The women agreed that it would, indeed, be splendid to have their own barrel, and even the men, when told of the project at night, were impressed by the difference in price when buying by the nine-gallon cask. Some of them worked it out on paper and were satisfied that, considering that they would be spending a few shillings extra at Christmas in any case, and that the missus had been looking rather peaked lately and a glass of good beer cost less than doctor's physic, and that maybe a daughter in service would be sending a postal order, they might venture to order the cask.

Others did not trouble to work it out; but, enchanted with the idea, gave the order lightheartedly. After all, as the outrider said, Christmas came but once a year, and this year they would have a jolly one. Of course there were kill-joys, like Laura's father, who said sardonically: "They'll laugh the other side of their faces when it comes to paying for it."

The barrels came and were tapped and the beer was handed around. The barrels were empty and the brewer's carter in his leather apron heaved them into the van behind his steaming, stamping horses; but none of the mustard or cocoa tins hidden away in secret places contained more than a few coppers towards paying the bill. When the day of reckoning came only three of the purchasers had the money ready. But time was allowed. Next month would do; but, mind! it must be forthcoming then. Most of the women tried hard to get that money together; but, of course, they could not. The traveller called again and again, each time growing more threatening, and, after some months, the brewer took the matter to the County Court, where the judge, after hearing the circumstances of sale and the income of the purchasers, ordered them all to pay twopence weekly off the debt. So ended the great excitement of having one's own barrel of beer on tap.

FLORA THOMPSON
Lark Rise 1939

19

Our greatest observance of custom is, as it should be, in connexion with Christmas-tide. Indeed preparation for the same really commences some weeks in advance. There is the pudding to make and partly boil; all the ingredients for the plum-cake to order; the mincemeat to prepare for the mince-pies; the goose to choose from some neighbouring farmer's stock; the cheese to buy; and the wheat to have hullins beaten out and to cree [stew], for the all-important frumenty; the Yule-cake or pepper-cake to make; the hollin to gather...

RICHARD BLAKEBOROUGH
A Yorkshire Farmer 1898

Get ivy and hull*, woman, deck up thine house,
And take this same brawn for to seethe and to souse;
Provide us good cheer, for thou knowest the old guise,
Old customs that good be, let no man despise.

* holly

THOMAS TUSSER
The Farmers' Daily Diet 1557
(Five Hundred Points of Good Husbandry)

Gradually there gathered the feeling of expectation. Christmas was coming. In the shed, at nights, a secret candle was burning, a sound of veiled voices was heard. The boys were learning the old mystery play of St. George and Beelzebub. Twice a week, by lamplight, there was choir practice in the church, for the learning of old carols. The girls went to these practices. Everywhere was a sense of mystery and rousedness. Everybody was preparing for something.

The time came near, the girls were decorating the church, with cold fingers binding holly and fir and yew about the pillars, till a new spirit was in the church, the stone broke out into dark, rich leaf, the arches put forth their buds, and cold flowers rose to blossom in the dim, mystic atmosphere. Ursula must weave mistletoe over the door, and over the screen, and hang a silver dove from a sprig of yew, till dusk came down, and the church was like a grove.

In the cowshed the boys were blacking their faces for a dress rehearsal; the turkey hung dead, with opened speckled wings, in the dairy. The time was come to make pies, in readiness.

D. H. LAWRENCE
The Rainbow 1915

It's getting nearly Christmas now. I dunno how long we got to wait, but it's pretty soon. The shop round the corner's selling these Christmas trees. They ain't got no lights on or nothing like that, but they're real nice all the same. If you stick your hand in them it's all prickly 'cos they got these tiny little leaf things and they prick. The best thing about them is their smell. They smell real good, I reckon.

I bought some Christmas cards all on my own. I went into this shop and got a little box of them. I was pretty pleased with myself. They're real nice cards – there's some that got pictures of a blue sky with a big white star and some men on a camel and that. And there's some of baby Jesus in his bed with all these cows and sheep and stuff looking at him all gentle like.

NIGEL WATTS
Billy Bayswater 1990

In the dining-room and drawing-room our decorations were confined to holly, but Cyril and I let ourselves go in the kitchen. We had bought at Cole's, for a few pence, coloured paper streamers that opened like a concertina. By joining several together these could be hung right across the kitchen ceiling. We dragged the kitchen table from side to side and climbed on it, fixing the streamers, rather precariously, with nails and pins. However, when we had finished, and were admiring the effect, Lizzie reluctantly agreed that it did look gay. She was not much in sympathy with our activities, and wanted to know who was going to clear up the mess we made.

I had sent off my Christmas cards: not many, but each of the Aunts had to have one; then of course Father and Mother (these were put by till tomorrow); and there were Gussie and Lizzie and her sisters. It was fortunate that I did not have to buy all these cards with my own meagre savings. Mother always kept such of last year's cards as had no writing on them, or only in pencil, and we were able to use these again. The pencil marks were erased, usually quite ineffectually, with a rather grubby piece of india-rubber, and a greeting written on top, heavily, and in ink, to help in the disguise. The procedure was fraught with dangers and I was only saved from disaster by Mother looking over my shoulder and saying, "Darling, you *can't* send that one to Aunt Alicia. It's the one she sent me last year."

ERNEST H. SHEPARD
Drawn from Memory 1957

The postman came through the wood with a bundle of letters and Christmas cards. He stood by the fire and had a cup of tea, and admired the decorations whilst Margaret opened her letters with cries of happiness, and excitement.

Susan had a card which she liked above everything, a church with roof and towers and foreground covered in glittering snow. But when it was held up to the light, colours streamed through the windows, reds and blues, from two patches at the back. She put it with her best treasures to be kept for ever.

ALISON UTTLEY
The Country Child 1931

The growing inclination to revive the old-fashioned Christmas within the present reign is strongly emphasised this year, when all the large country houses are crowded with guests. Christmas trees for young and old, dances, theatricals, children's parties, hunting meets, breakfasts and balls, and entertainments for the servants and tenantry are all included in the programme for the observance of the festival.

The King and Queen have set the example, and the Sandringham party at this season is that of a typical English home. Their Majesties have surrounded themselves with friends, and there is a giant Christmas tree laden with gifts for every member of the party, as well as toys and instructive games for the Royal grandchildren. Every article is chosen with due regard to the age and tastes of the recipient, and Queen Alexandra personally superintends the distribution.

The Prince and Princess of Wales left London on Saturday to join their children at York Cottage. Prince Edward, with his brothers and Princess Mary, look forward eagerly to the Christmas festival, and Santa Claus has as much interest for them as for children of humbler rank. A special Christmas tree is provided for the young princes, whose favourite toys are motor-boats and trains, and other mechanical contrivances. The old wooden rocking-horse so much in request a generation ago is as dead as the dodo, and is superseded by fat elephants which are "warranted safe and quiet to ride", and are the popular mounts of the two youngest princes.

December has been an exciting month for the Prince of Wales's children, all of whom have been busy contriving presents for their parents and grandparents. Great secrecy prevails in the Royal nursery as to the precise nature of the work in hand. Princess Mary is, as usual, the leader of these small conspiracies to provide surprise gifts. The little princess is expert with the knitting and crochet needles. She turns out a regular stock of well-made silk ties for her father and her uncles, as well as motor scarves, one of which the King received as a birthday gift.

Their Majesties' Christmas
Daily Chronicle 1905

Come, bring with a noise,
My merrie merrie boyes,
The Christmas Log to the firing;
Whilst my good Dame, she
Bids ye all be free;
And drink to your hearts desiring.

With the last yeares brand
Light the new block, and
For good successe in his spending,
On your Psaltries play,
That sweet luck may
Come while the log is a-teending.

Drink now the strong Beere,
Cut the white loafe here,
The while the meat is a-shredding;
For the rare Mince-Pie,
And the Plums stand by
To fill the paste that's a-kneading.

ROBERT HERRICK (1591-1674)
Ceremonies for Christmas

Kindle the Christmas brand, and then
Till sunset let it burn;
Which quench'd, then lay it up again,
Till Christmas next return.

Part must be kept wherewith to teend
The Christmas log next year;
And where 'tis safely kept, the fiend
Can do no mischief there.

ROBERT HERRICK (1591-1674)
Another Ceremony for Christmas

3
The Town Gets Ready

As the month drew on the thought of the stars was in everyone's minds, for Christmas was coming in in the traditional way, with frost and snow upon the ground and such a blaze of constellations in the night sky that it seemed the heavens were hanging low over the earth in most unusual friendliness.

And certainly the city of Oxford was good to look at at this time. By day, under a brilliant blue sky, the gabled roofs and tall chimneys, the towers and spires, took on an added brightness from the tracery of sparkling frost that clung to them; and down below them the narrow streets were bright with the bunchy little figures of snowballing children, happy girls and beaming mothers going shopping with baskets on their arms, dressed in their gaudiest because it was Christmas-time, and laughing men with sprigs of holly in their caps, their faces as rosy as apples from the potations they had partaken of at the taverns and inns in honour of the festive season. The bad smells of the town had been obliterated by the continual snow showers and the hard frost – it would be a different story when the thaw came, but sufficient unto the day is the evil thereof – and delicious festive scents floated out into the streets from open doors and windows; scents of baked meats and roasting apples, of ale and wine, of spices and perfumes and the fragrant wood-smoke from innumerable fires of apple-wood and beech-logs and resinous pine-branches. And at night the city seemed almost as brilliant as the starry sky above. From sheer goodwill doors were left ajar and windows uncurtained, so that bright beams of light lay aslant across the shadows, and the gay groups that thronged the streets carried lanterns that bobbed like fireflies over the trampled snow. The bells rang out continuously and the laughter and clear voices of the children made unceasing music.

ELIZABETH GOUDGE
Towers in the Mist 1936

The darkness throbbed with the clamour of church bells. The six sonorous voices of St. Patrick's peal chased each other, now in regular rhythm, now in staccato clashes, as the bell-ringers sweated at their Christmas peal practice.

The night was iron-cold. Frost glittered on the hedges and fields of Fairacre although it was not yet eight o'clock. Thatched roofs were furred with white rime beneath a sky brilliant with stars. Smoke rose in unwavering blue wisps from cottage chimneys, for the air was uncannily still. The sound of the bells carried far in such weather.

MISS READ
Village Christmas 1966

The little town of Lulling was beginning to deck itself in its Christmas finery. In the market square a tall Christmas tree towered, its dark branches threaded with electric lights. At night it twinkled with red, blue, yellow and orange pinpoints of colour and gladdened the hearts of all the children.

The shop windows sported snow scenes, Christmas bells, paper chains and reindeer. The window of the local electricity showroom had a life-size tableau of a family at Christmas dinner, which was much admired. Wax figures, with somewhat yellow and jaundiced complexions, sat smiling glassily at a varnished papier mâché turkey, their forks upraised in happy anticipation. Upon their straw-like hair were perched paper hats of puce and lime green, and paper napkins, ablaze with holly sprigs, were tucked into their collars. The fact that they were flanked closely by a washing machine, a spin dryer and a refrigerator did not appear to disturb them.

With only a fortnight to go before Christmas Day Lulling people were beginning to bestir themselves about their shopping. London might start preparing for the festival at the end of October; Lulling refused to be hustled. October and November had jobs of their own in plenty. December, and the latter part at that, was the proper time to think of Christmas, and the idea of buying cards and presents before then was just plain silly.

But now all the good folk were ready for it, and the shops did a brisk trade. Baskets bulged, and harassed matrons struggled along the crowded main street bearing awkward objects like tricycles and pairs of stilts, flimsily wrapped in flapping paper. Children kept up a shrill piping for the tawdry knick-knacks which caught their eye, and fathers gazed speculatively at train sets and wondered if their two-year-old sons and daughters would be a good excuse to buy one.

MISS READ
Winter in Thrush Green 1961

The electric shop down the road's got these fairy lights in the window. You know, for Christmas, like. They leave them on all night, even when the shop's shut. It's real great to watch them 'cos they blink on and off all the time. They're all round the window. They don't half look pretty.

Marie says there's a street in town that's all lit up with Christmas lights – you know, all across the street and that. She says she might take me to see them. I'd really like that, I would – I really like Christmassy things.

Then some music starts up. It's coming from outside, so I go out and have a look. There's this big brass band set up in the middle of the station with these people sitting in chairs with their instruments all silvery and shiny. It sounds really nice, the music they're making – it's all loud and echoey. They're playing Christmas songs – I know 'cos I heard this one at school before. I go right up so I can see proper. They're all wearing the same sort of clothes – black, with these black hats – even the girls. I like the man who's playing this great big shiny thing like a fog horn. I listen real close to him, but he don't really play the tune – he just sort of goes blah-blah-blah every now and then. It don't really sound like the tune, but it fits in real well with the rest of them.

A girl in a smart black uniform is collecting money in this box and quite a few people stop and drop money in it. I wish I had some money to give her, but I ain't got none left.

The next song they play is a slow one – Silent Night. It's one of my favourites. We used to sing this one at school. It's all about baby Jesus being born and that. I wish I could remember the words, but I've forgot them so I just hum along with the tune.

The band plays for quite a bit. I know most of the songs, but there's one or two I don't. They're nice songs – even the ones I don't know. I specially like the man with the big silvery fog horn thing. I'd like to play one of them.

When they finish, the band pack up and fold their chairs up. There's lots of talking and laughing when they do that – they look like they've had a real good time. I just sort of hang around watching them. A big van pulls up and they stick their stuff inside and get in, but just before they go, the man with the fog horn thing turns round and says all friendly like, "Happy Christmas". I say "Happy Christmas" back and then he gets into the van and they drive off.

NIGEL WATTS
Billy Bayswater 1990

4
The End of Term

Preparations for Christmas are now in full swing. For weeks past the shops in Caxley have been a blaze of coloured lights and decorated with Father Christmases, decked trees, silver balls and all the other paraphernalia. Even our grocer's shop in Fairacre has cotton-wool snow, hanging on threads, down the window, and this, and the crib already set up in the church all add to the children's enchantment.

Yesterday afternoon the whole school was busy making Christmas decorations and Christmas cards. There is nothing that children like more than making brightly-coloured paper chains, and their tongues wagged happily as the paste brushes were plied, and yet another glowing link was added to the festoons that lay piled up on the floor. All this glory grows so deliciously quickly and the knowledge that, very soon, it will be swinging aloft, above our heads, among the pitch-pine rafters – an enchanting token of all the joys that Christmas holds in store – makes them work with more than usual energy.

In Miss Jackson's room the din was terrific, so excited were the chain-makers. The only quiet group here was the one which was composed of about eight small children who had elected to crayon Christmas cards instead.

MISS READ
Village Diary 1957

The lights came on and there was the manger and Mary and Joseph. Shepherds were lounging a little way away, where the angel made his third appearance, illumined by powerful beams, and cried, "Fear not!" and they all fell down. A heavenly choir joined him in song. Wise men appeared, coming up the aisle, uncertain whether they were doing the right thing. "Where is he that is born King of the Jews? For we have seen his star in the east and are come to worship him." They met the gang of shepherds going west and all went in together and knelt down at the manger. Gifts were given, prayers said, and some of the shepherds remembered most of the long prophetic passage from Isaiah. "Behold the Lamb of God, who taketh away the sins of the world," one said.

And then silence. The children huddled together on their knees, heads bowed, such a peaceful sight and yet you wondered if it was the end or what came next – nobody moved, Mary and Joseph knelt like statues, nobody said a word. They remained in perfect adoration until the organ began to play and then, remembering that it was time to go, they got up and left and the pageant was over.

GARRISON KEILLOR
Lake Wobegon Days 1985

The property box furnished us with a considerable amount of the costumes required. Mr. Roberts, the local farmer and a school governor, provided hay for the box which represented the manger. The ox and the ass had been cut out of heavy cardboard years before, and had weathered their sojourn stuffed behind the map cupboard with remarkable endurance. Once dusted, and an eye re-drawn, they were as good as new, we told each other.

The shepherds were clothed in dressing gowns, but here again it was quite a job to find suitably subfusc attire. Gaily patterned bath robes were paraded before us, sporting dragons, Disney characters and a panda or two. Where, I wondered, were the old-fashioned boys' camel-coloured numbers which I remembered from my youth?

After much searching we found one or two, and reckoned that the wardrobe and properties were at last complete.

We gave our first performance one afternoon in the last week of term. I was very grateful to the vicar for letting us have the beautiful chancel for our stage. Usually, any end of term function takes place in Fairacre school, and we are obliged to force back the wooden and glass partition between the two classrooms to make one large hall. Then there is the usual scurrying about for chairs from the school-house and public-spirited nearby neighbours, not to mention some rickety benches from the village hall and the cricket pavilion which arrive on a trailer of Mr. Roberts', and have to be manhandled into place for the great event, and manhandled back again to their usual home.

On this occasion our audience sat in the ancient pews and had a clear view of the chancel. Mr. Bennett, the foster-father at the first Trust's home, had emerged as an electrical wizard, and had volunteered to arrange temporary lighting. This threw the stage into sharp contrast with the dimness of the surrounding building, and gave the performance a wonderfully dramatic setting.

The play went without many hitches. At one point, the cardboard ox fell down in a sudden draught from the vestry door, and Joseph's crêpe beard came adrift from one ear. This, however, was replaced swiftly by one of the shepherds, hissing "stand still, stand still!" whilst adjusting the wire over his classmate's left ear, and we all waited for the performance to continue.

It would not have been right to have a school affair like this without some minor mishap, and we all thoroughly enjoyed ourselves.

The vicar closed the proceedings with a suitable prayer, and we filed out into the misty afternoon feeling all the better for celebrating, in our homespun way, the birth of Jesus.

MISS READ
Farewell to Fairacre 1993

Mrs. Smith, the head teacher, had invited me to stay to see the children's Nativity play. This was to be the fourth one I'd seen within a fortnight and every one had been quite different from the last.

Mary, a pretty little thing of about six or seven, was busy bustling about the stage dusting, when the Angel of the Lord appeared stage right. The heavenly spirit was a tall self-conscious boy with a plain, pale face and sticking out ears. He was dressed in a flowing white robe with large paper wings and sported a crooked tinsel halo. Having wiped his nose on his sleeve, he glanced around suspiciously and sidled up to Mary, like a dodgy market trader seeing if you were interested in buying something "under the counter".

"Who are you?" Mary asked sharply, putting down her duster and placing her hands on her hips. This was not the quietly-spoken, gentle-natured Mary I was used to. — —

When the Angel of the Lord departed, Joseph entered, a cheeky-faced little boy dressed in a brown dressing gown, thick blue socks and a multi-coloured towel on his head, held in place by the inevitable elastic belt with a snake clasp. — —

We now move to the final scene. Children began to enter the stage from both sides and gather round the baby. The whole area was now filled with children singing Away in a Manger in clear high voices. When the carol had finished, I sat for a moment and looked around me. The children's faces were glowing with pleasure. Mrs Smith was wiping away a tear, the lights of the fir tree twinkled and the walls were ablaze with the colours of Christmas. Through the classroom window a pale sun cast a translucent light on the countryside and the whole world gleamed silver. This, I thought, was indeed something spiritual.

GERVASE PHINN
Over Hill and Dale 2000

My first day there was just before Christmas, so that at the start I had the pill gilded by seeing the school-rooms decorated with paper-chains and tinsel stars. The hall loomed up huge and dark in the winter gloom of a Battersea December. My timid wits congealed, and I moved as though I were wholly in a world of nightmare. The floor appeared to be covered by files of children, winding in and out under the guiding hands of several grown-ups, to the thumping tune from a piano, while the decorations overhead swung in the foggy height.

All that I recollect now of that first day at school is a scene of vastness: the enormous hall, the class-rooms, the endless files of children constantly on the move; the big Christmas tree and the grey-haired figure standing by it, handing out gifts taken from its sugary twigs as another woman shouted numbers.

Bewildered by the psychological novelty, and the physical strangeness of large spaces and huge numbers, I found myself being pushed forward to the tree, and taking from the old lady a sugar pig. It had a pink-mauve snout, and a blue ribbon round its neck. Its hide sparkled, hard and crystalline.

RICHARD CHURCH
Over the Bridge 1955

The last day of term, particularly the Christmas term, has a splendour all of its own. There is an air of excitement at the thought of pleasures and freedom to come, but there is also a feeling of relaxation from daily routine made much more acute by the deliciously empty desks. Books have been collected and stacked in neat piles in the cupboard. Papers and exercise books have been tidied away. All that remains to employ young hands in this last glorious day is a pencil and loose sheets of paper which have been saved for just such an occasion.

Of course, work will be done. There will be mental arithmetic, and some writing; perhaps some spelling lists and paper games, and stories told to each other. And today, the children knew, there would be Christmas carols, and a visit to the old grey church next door to see the crib recently set up by the vicar's wife and other ladies of the village. The very thought of it all created a glow which warmed the children despite the winter's cold.

MISS READ
Over the Gate 1964

It was the last afternoon and the Christmas party was in full swing. Lemonade glasses were empty, paper hats askew, and the children's faces flushed with excitement. They sat at their disordered tables, which were their workaday desks, pushed up together in fours and camouflaged with Christmas table-cloths. Their eyes were fixed on the Christmas tree in the centre of the room, glittering and sparkling with frosted baubles and tinsel. The pink and blue parcels dangled temptingly and a cheer went up as the vicar advanced with the school cutting-out scissors.

The floor was a welter of paper, bent straws and crumbs, and I saw Mrs. Pringle's mouth drooping down, tortoise-fashion, as she surveyed the wreckage. Luckily the vicar clapped his hands for silence before she had a chance for any damping remark.

MISS READ
Village School 1955

Let me begin with the Christmas treat at the school. It was always held on the day we broke up for the holidays. All pretence of work stopped at noon when we were set free for an hour's play in the open. Suddenly the bell rang. The din halted for a moment of intense silence, for even the wind seemed to hold its breath. Then we all rushed for the schoolroom and the Feed.

The next four hours were the one time of the year when the school wore any aspect of true humanity. The sliding partition had been opened, throwing the two rooms into one, and revealing the total splendour of the decorations. It was a riot of coloured paper, evergreens and holly berries. The big table in the Infant room bore a noble array of tea-urns and cups, while another supported a rare assortment of fancy cooking. Odd hampers stood about full of luscious exciting things that would be revealed in due course.

It was with the greatest difficulty that we could be persuaded into our places. When we had been reduced to order, our mothers and sisters found seats on the benches where most of them had learned the ABC in their day.

Miss Thom opened the piano; Miss Grey banged the floor with her pointer; and the company rose and burst into full-throated melody about "When humble shepherds watched their flocks". After the angels had been

33

assumed back to Heaven, with a distressing uncertainty as to tone among the older boys, we chanted the Lord's Prayer with unusual heartiness and then broke into a clatter of excitement.

Two ladies appeared with the tea. Others distributed bags of cakes. The Grand Feed began. Each child received a bag of buns and a mutton-pie, which had to be eaten before the more interesting sweets came round. We were not fastidious. Our rural appetites had not been corrupted by éclairs. We fell on the rather sober pastries with happy shouts and washed them down with cupfuls of hot sweet tea. It was a heartening sight, with sixty feeding as one.

When we had finished the plain fare and burst all the bags, after much misdirected expenditure of wind, the mothers and sisters handed round their baskets of home bakeries – jam puffs, almond cakes, shortbread and sugared biscuits. And still the wonder grew that we didn't burst. But Nature beat us at last and we had to give up.

JOHN R. ALLAN
Farmer's Boy 1935

5
Going the Rounds

The week before Christmas, when snow seemed to lie thickest, was the moment for carol-singing; and when I think back to those nights it is to the crunch of snow and to the lights of the lanterns on it.

"Coming carol-barking then?"

We were the Church Choir, so no answer was necessary. For a year we had praised the Lord out of key, and as a reward for this service – on top of the Outing – we now had the right to visit all the big houses, to sing our carols and to collect our tribute.

Our first call as usual was the house of the Squire, and we trouped nervously down his drive. For light we had candles in marmalade-jars suspended on loops of string, and they threw pale gleams on the towering snowdrifts that stood on each side of the drive. A blizzard was blowing, but we were well wrapped up, with Army puttees on our legs, woollen hats on our heads, and several scarves around our ears.

As we sang "Wild Shepherds" we craned our necks, gaping into the lamplit hall which we had never entered; staring at the muskets and un-tenanted chairs, the great tapestries furred by dust – until suddenly, on the stairs, we saw the old Squire himself standing and listening with his head on one side.

He didn't move until we'd finished; then slowly he tottered towards us, dropped two coins in our box with a trembling hand, scratched his name in the book we carried, gave us each a long look with his moist blind eyes, then turned away in silence.

As though released from a spell, we took a few sedate steps, then broke into a run for the gate. We didn't stop till we were out of the grounds. Im-patient, at least, to discover the extent of his bounty, we squatted by the cowsheds, held our lanterns over the book, and saw that he had written "Two Shillings". This was quite a good start. No one of any worth in the district would dare to give us less than the Squire.

Steadily we worked through the length of the valley, going from house to house, visiting the lesser and the greater gentry. Mile after mile we went, fighting against the wind, falling into snowdrifts, and navigating by the lights of the houses.

We approached our last house high up on the hill. Everything was quiet; everywhere there was the faint crackling silence of the winter night. We started singing, and we were all moved by the words and the sudden trueness of our voices. Pure, very clear and breathless we sang. And two thousand Christmases became real to us then.

LAURIE LEE
Cider with Rosie 1959

And I remember that we went singing carols once, a night or two before Christmas Eve, when there wasn't the shaving of a moon to light the secret, white-flying streets. At the end of a long road was a drive that led to a large house, and we stumbled up the darkness of the drive that night, each one of us afraid, each one holding a stone in his hand in case, and all of us too brave to say a word. The wind made through the drive-trees noises as of old and unpleasant and maybe web-footed men wheezing in caves. We reached the black bulk of the house.

"What shall we give them?" Dan whispered. "Hark the Herald?"

"No," Jack said. "We'll sing Good King Wenceslas. I'll count three."

One, two, three, and we began to sing, our voices high and seemingly distant in the snow-felted darkness round the house that was occupied by nobody we knew. We stood close together, near the door.

Good King Wenceslas looked out
On the feast of Stephen.

And then a small, dry voice, like the voice of someone who has not spoken for a long time, suddenly joined our singing: a small dry voice from the other side of the door: a small dry voice through the keyhole.

DYLAN THOMAS
A Child's Christmas in Wales
(Published posthumously 1955)

36

Shortly after ten o'clock the singing-boys arrived at the tranter's house, which was invariably the place of meeting, and preparations were made for the start. The older men and musicians wore thick coats, with stiff perpendicular collars, and coloured handkerchiefs wound round and round the neck till the end came to hand, over all which they just showed their ears and noses, like people looking over a wall. The remainder, stalwart ruddy men and boys, were dressed mainly in snow-white smock-frocks, embroidered upon the shoulders and breasts in ornamental forms of hearts, diamonds, and zig-zags. The cider-mug was emptied for the ninth time, the music-books were arranged, and the pieces finally decided upon. The boys in the meantime put the old horn-lanterns in order, cut candles into short lengths to fit the lanterns; and, a thin fleece of snow having fallen since the early part of the evening, those who had no leggings went to the stable and wound wisps of hay round their ankles to keep the insidious flakes from the interior of their boots.

Melstock was a parish of considerable acreage, the hamlets composing it lying at a much greater distance from each other than is ordinarily the case. Hence several hours were consumed in playing and singing within hearing of every family, even if but a single air were bestowed on each.

Old William Dewy, with the violoncello, played the bass; his grandson Dick the treble violin; and Reuben and Michael Mail the tenor and second violins respectively. The singers consisted of four men and seven boys, upon whom devolved the task of carrying and attending to the lanterns, and holding the books open for the players. Directly music was the theme old William ever and instinctively came to the front.

"Now mind, neighbours," he said, as they all went out one by one at the door, he himself holding it ajar and regarding them with a critical face as they passed, like a shepherd counting out his sheep. "You two counter-boys, keep your ears open to Michael's fingering, and don't ye go straying into the treble part along o' Dick and his set, as ye did last year; and mind this especially when we be in "Arise, and hail". Billy Chimlen, don't you sing quite so raving mad as you fain would; and, all o' ye, whatever ye do, keep from making a great scuffle on the ground when we go in at people's gates; but go quietly, so as to strike up all of a sudden, like spirits. And, Voss," said the tranter terminatively, "you keep house here till about half-past two; then heat the metheglin and cider in the warmer you'll find turned up upon the copper; and bring it wi' the victuals to church-hatch, as th'st know."

Just before the clock struck twelve they lighted the lanterns and started. The moon, in her third quarter, had risen since the snowstorm; but the dense accumulation of snow-cloud weakened her power to a faint twilight which was rather pervasive of the landscape than traceable to the sky. The breeze had gone down, and the rustle of their feet and tones of their speech echoed with an alert rebound from every post, boundary-stone, and ancient wall they passed, even where the distance of the echo's origin was less than a few yards. Beyond their own slight noises nothing was to be heard save the occasional bark of foxes in the direction of Yalbury Wood, or the brush of a rabbit among the grass now and then as it scampered out of their way.

Most of the outlying homesteads and hamlets had been visited by about two o'clock; they then passed across the out-skirts of a wooded park toward the main village, nobody being at home at the Manor. Pursuing no recognized track, great care was necessary in walking lest their faces should come in contact with the low-hanging boughs of the old lime-trees, which in many spots formed dense overgrowths of interlaced branches.

"Times have changed from the times they used to be," said Mail. "People don't care much about us now! I've been thinking we must be almost the last left in the county of the old string players? Barrel-organs, and the things next door to 'em that you blow wi' your foot, have come in terribly of late years."

By this time they were crossing to a gate in the direction of the school which, standing on a slight eminence at the junction of three ways, now rose in unvarying and dark flatness against the sky. The instruments were retuned, and all the band entered the school enclosure, enjoined by old William to keep upon the grass.

"Number seventy-eight," he softly gave out as they formed round in a semicircle, the boys opening the lanterns to get a clearer light, and directing their rays on the books.

Then passed forth into the quiet night an ancient and time-worn hymn, embodying a quaint Christianity in words orally transmitted from father to son through several generations down to the present characters, who sang them out right earnestly.

Having concluded the last note they listened for a minute or two, but found that no sound issued from the schoolhouse.

"Four breaths, and then the last," said the leader authoritatively. "Rejoice, ye Tenants of the Earth, number sixty-four."

At the close, waiting yet another minute, he said in a clear, loud voice, as he had said in the village at that hour and season for the previous forty years – "A merry Christmas to ye!"

They now crossed Melstock Bridge, and went along an embowered path beside the Froom towards the church and vicarage, meeting Voss with the hot mead and bread-and-cheese as they were approaching the churchyard. This determined them to eat and drink before proceeding further, and they entered the church and ascended to the gallery. The lanterns were opened, and the whole body sat round against the walls on benches and whatever else was available, and made a hearty meal. In the pauses of conversation there could be heard through the floor overhead a little world of undertones and creaks from the halting clockwork, which never spread further than the tower they were born in, and raised in the more meditative minds a fancy that here lay the direct pathway of Time.

THOMAS HARDY
Under the Greenwood Tree 1872

6
The Tree

We didn't have Christmas trees up here in Northumberland. I don't know if they were too poor or what, but we didn't have Christmas trees, so you used to try and find a nice holly tree out in the wood. And you used to keep your eye on that holly tree and, when it came time, before Christmas, if you were lucky enough you were able to cut it. But if somebody beat you, well, you didn't get one. Then what we used to do, we used to decorate it, put streamers down, make it lifelike, and we'd hang all these little toys until you got your tree absolutely covered. And then at night you used to put it in the window where people could see it. And it was a grand thing for people to come in and see who had the best tree; it was like a competition.

ALF TODD (in service)
Approx 1914-18
(Christmas Past, Gavin Weightman and Steve Humphries)

How well I remember the Christmases at Hallingbury Place, a massive country house. They used to have all the villagers, the men who worked on the estate, all fourteen gardeners, grooms and laundry people (they had their own laundry) all around the Christmas tree. I can see the old gardener now. They used to drag the tree in, and it used to go right up to the top of the ceiling in this massive old servants' hall. The room was packed. I stood and watched the whole procedure. They were really happy these people; it was pleasant to see them enjoying themselves.

CHARLES DE'ATH (in service)
Approx 1914-18 (Christmas Past, Gavin Weightman and Steve Humphries)

A young fir is generally selected and little presents of various kinds are bound on the branches, crochet-purses, bonbons, preserved fruits, alum-baskets, charms, dolls, toys in endless variety etc., distributed over the tree according to fancy. The whole is illuminated by numerous little wax tapers, which are lighted just before the guests are admitted to inspect the tree.

The Dictionary of Daily Wants 1858

Two men-servants in full livery came and carried the fir-tree into a fine big room. Portraits hung round the walls, and by the great tiled stove stood large Chinese vases with lions on their lids. There were rocking-chairs, silk-covered sofas, great tables full of picture-books and covered with toys worth hundreds and hundreds of pounds - at least, that's what the children said. And the fir-tree was set up in a big tub filled with sand, but no one could see it was a tub because it was draped all round with green cloth and stood on a large brightly-coloured carpet. Oh, how the tree trembled! Whatever would happen now? Men-servants and young ladies came and decorated it; they hung little baskets cut out of coloured paper on the branches, and every basket was filled with sweets. Gilded apples and walnuts were hung up and looked as if they were growing there; and over a hundred little candles, red, blue, and white, were fastened firmly to the branches. Dolls that looked really life-like – the tree had never seen anything like them before – swayed among the green needles, and right at the very top of the tree a big gold-tinsel star was fixed. It was magnificent, perfectly magnificent.

"This evening," they all said, "this evening it will be a blaze of light!"

Oh, thought the tree, if only it were evening! If only the candles were lit! And what will happen then, I wonder? I wonder if the trees will come from the forest to look at me? Will the sparrows fly up to the window? Shall I take root here and stand decorated, summer and winter?

Yes, it could think of nothing else — — —

Now the candles were lit. What radiance! What magnificence! The tree was so excited by it that all its branches quivered.

HANS CHRISTIAN ANDERSEN (1805-1875)
The Fir Tree

I have been looking on, this evening, at a merry company of children assembled round that pretty German toy, a Christmas Tree. The tree was planted in the middle of a great round table, and towered high above their heads. It was brilliantly lighted by a multitude of little tapers; and everywhere sparkled and glittered with bright objects. There were rosy-cheeked dolls, hiding behind the green leaves; and there were real watches (with movable hands, at least, and an endless capacity of being wound up) dangling from innumerable twigs; there were French-polished tables, chairs, bedsteads, wardrobes, eight-day clocks and various other articles of domestic furniture (wonderfully made, in tin, at Wolverhampton), perched among the boughs, as if in preparation for some fairy house-keeping; there were jolly, broad-faced little men, much more agreeable in appearance than many real men – and no wonder, for their heads took off, and showed them to be full of sugar-plums; there were fiddles and drums; there were tambourines, books, work-boxes, paint-boxes, sweetmeat-boxes, peepshow-boxes, and all kinds of boxes; there were trinkets for the elder girls, far brighter than any grown-up gold and jewels; there were baskets and pin-cushions in all devices; there were guns, swords, and banners; there were witches standing in enchanted rings of pasteboard, to tell fortunes; there were teetotums, humming-tops, needle-cases, pen-wipers, smelling-bottles, conversation-cards, bouquet-holders; real fruit, made artificially dazzling with gold leaf; imitation apples, pears and walnuts, crammed with surprises; in short, as a pretty child, before me, delightedly whispered to another pretty child, her bosom friend, "There was everything, and more". This motley collection of odd objects, clustering on the tree like magic fruit, and flashing back the bright looks directed towards it from every side – some of the diamond-eyes admiring it were hardly on a level with the table, and a few were languishing in timid wonder on the bosoms of pretty mothers, aunts, and nurses – made a lively realisation of the fancies of childhood; and set me thinking how all the trees that grow and all the things that come into existence on the earth, have their wild adornments at that well-remembered time.

CHARLES DICKENS
Household Words 1850

The Christmas tree in the engraving is that which is annually prepared by her Majesty's command for the Royal children. The tree employed for this festive purpose is a young fir of about eight feet high, and has six tiers of branches. On each tier, or branch, are arranged a dozen wax tapers. Pendant from the branches are elegant trays, baskets, bonbonnières, and other receptacles for sweetmeats of the most varied and expensive kind; and of all forms, colours and degrees of beauty. Fancy cakes, gilt gingerbread and eggs filled with sweetmeats, are also suspended by variously coloured ribbons from the branches. The tree, which stands upon a table covered with white damask, is supported at the root by piles of sweets of a larger kind, and by toys and dolls of all descriptions, suited to the youthful fancy, and to the several ages of the interesting scions of royalty for whose gratification they are displayed.

Illustrated London News
Queen Victoria's Tree 1848

Put out the lights now!
Look at the Tree, the rough tree dazzled
In oriole plumes of flame,
Tinselled with twinkling frost fire, tasselled
With stars and moons – the same
That yesterday hid in the spinney and had no fame
Till we put out the lights now.

Hard are the nights now:
The fields at moonrise turn to agate,
Shadows are cold as jet;
In dyke and furrow, in copse and faggot
The frost's tooth is set;
And stars are the sparks whirled out by the north wind's fret

On the flinty nights now.

So feast your eyes now
On mimic star and moon-cold bauble:
Worlds may wither unseen,
But the Christmas Tree is a tree of fable,
A phoenix in evergreen,
And the world cannot change or chill what its mysteries mean
To your hearts and eyes now.

C. DAY LEWIS
The Christmas Tree 1935

The kindly Christmas tree, from which I trust every gentle reader has pulled a bonbon or two, is yet all aflame whilst I am writing, and sparkles with the sweet fruits of its season. You young ladies, may you have plucked pretty giftlings from it; and out of the cracker sugar-plum which you have split with the captain or the sweet young curate may you have read one of those delicious conundrums which the confectioners introduce into the sweetmeats, and which apply to the cunning passion of Love. Those riddles are to be read at *your* age, when I dare say they are amusing. As for Dolly, Merry, and Bell, who are standing at the tree, they don't care about the love-riddle part, but understand the sweet-almond portion very well. They are four, five, six years old. Patience, little people! A dozen merry Christmasses more, and you will be reading those wonderful love-conundrums, too.

W. M. THACKERAY (1811-1863)
The Sparkling Bough

In twenty of the slummiest districts of London nearly three thousand of the poorest of children have experienced the delight of gazing upon a Christmas tree, and receiving some gifts from its toy laden boughs. The little ones were standing around the Christmas tree in a very intoxication of merriment.

The day following, the slum children marched about, filling the air with the sound of trumpet and mouth-organ. The girls paraded the courts with their new dolls, and thus they continued the rejoicing of the previous night. One little mite expressed the pent-up feelings of the rest by saying, as she hugged her dolly to her: "Oh sister! Wasn't it grand?"

SALVATION ARMY
Social Gazette 1900

One of my most important jobs was to walk round the tree with a wet sponge on the top of a pole, and as the candles burnt down I used to put them out safely with the wet sponge, thereby doing away with the risk of fire. Fire was an ever-present hazard in a place like Sherborne Castle with its valuable paintings. The staff used to come and line up in front of the tree, and Mrs. Wingfield-Digby used to give each one a present and I'd wander round the tree, not paying any attention to anyone else until the whole little ceremony was finished and all the candles were out.

JACK GOSNEY (in service)
Approx 1914-18 (Christmas Past, Gavin Weightman and Steve Humphries)

7
Christmas Eve

In the course of a December tour in Yorkshire, I rode for a long distance in one of the public coaches, on the day preceding Christmas. The coach was crowded, both inside and out, with passengers, who, by their talk, seemed principally bound to the mansions of relations or friends, to eat the Christmas dinner. It was loaded also with hampers of game, and baskets and boxes of delicacies; and hares hung dangling their long ears about the coachman's box, presents from distant friends for the impending feast. I had three fine rosy-cheeked school boys for my fellow passengers inside, full of the buxom health and manly spirit which I have observed in the children of this country. They were returning home for the holydays, in high glee, and promising themselves a world of enjoyment.

I could not but notice the more than ordinary air of bustle and importance of the coachman, who wore his hat a little on one side, and had a large bunch of Christmas greens stuck in the button hole of his coat. He is always a personage full of mighty care and business, but he is particularly so during this season, having so many commissions to execute in consequence of the great interchange of presents.

Perhaps the impending holyday might have given a more than usual animation to the country, for it seemed to me as if every body was in good looks and good spirits; game, poultry, and other luxuries of the table, were in brisk circulation in the villages; the grocer's, butcher's, and fruiterer's shops were thronged with customers. The housewives were stirring briskly about, putting their dwellings in order, and the glossy branches of holly, with their bright red berries, began to appear at the windows.

WASHINGTON IRVING
Sketch Book 1820

By the Christmas of 1904 I was a fully-fledged party-goer. The thrill of a party began the night before when my mother took special care over putting my hair in curl-rags. Every curl that was not quite tight enough was done again and I did not complain if the tightness was uncomfortable, it was part of the excitement. I cannot now imagine how I managed to sleep with those hard knobs, like glossy chestnuts from each of which sprouted a flutter of white curl-rag, all over my head. Next day time hung heavily until the afternoon when, on being told by my mother that everything was ready, I would steal upstairs, open the bedroom door very quietly, and gloat. The fire would be burning brightly and on the bed would be my party dress (always pink chiffon), a pink cloth hooded cape, a white wool shawl to go over it, bronze slippers, white silk openwork stockings, white silk mittens and a choice of three fans – ostrich feather, hand-painted or lace.

DODIE SMITH
Look Back with Love 1974

"The Players!" cried voices in the crowd. "The Christmas Players! The Players are here!"

He was only just in time, for as he flung himself into the crowd that streamed in beneath the archway the clear note of a trumpet told him that the performance was about to begin.

It was very crude and at some other time Nicolas might have been moved to mirth, but he was not so moved to-night, neither he nor a single man, woman or child in that densely packed throng. It was Christmas Eve, and the same stars shone above them as had shone upon the fields of Palestine some fifteen hundred years ago. They sat in a deep and lovely silence, their eyes riveted upon the rough wooden stage where the figures of shepherds moved, and angels whose dresses had shrunk in the wash and whose wings and haloes had become a little battered by so much packing and unpacking, and a Virgin Mary whose blue cloak was torn and whose voice was that of a young English peasant boy who had not so long ago been taken from the plough.

Wedged against the balustrade of the gallery, Nicolas watched and listened in that state of heavenly concentration that leaves the human creature oblivious of himself. He was not conscious any more of the apprentices who pressed upon him, or of the smell of unwashed human bodies, or of his own empty stomach that had been presented with no supper that evening. He was only dimly aware of the crowd as a great multitude that he could not number, watchers in the shadows who had been watching there for fifteen hundred years. The Christmas story itself absorbed him. Though it was so old a story, one that he had known as soon as he was capable of knowing anything, it seemed to-night quite new to him. "Glory to God in the highest….. A child is born." The old words he had heard a hundred times over seemed to cry out with the triumph of new and startling news. The figures that moved before him, Mary with the child in her arms, Joseph and the shepherds, Herod and the Wise Men, that he had seen so many times pictured in stained-glass windows and on the leaves of missals, moved now in this tiny space at the heart of the crowd as though they had come there for the first time…The love of God is with man… That, Nicolas knew suddenly, is the news of the far country, the mystery like a nugget of gold that men travel so far to seek, the fact that is stated but not explained, by all the pictures that have been painted and by all the music and the poetry that has been written since the dawn of the world. It was as easy as that, and as difficult

ELIZABETH GOUDGE
Towers in the Mist 1936

Christmas Eve was crisp and cold and bright and we were going carol singing in the evening, so I wanted to have mince-pies and sausage rolls ready to contribute to what we would all scoff afterwards. The kitchen was smelling wonderfully aromatic, of warm pastry and brandy and mincemeat, and it was very hot too.

The first batch of pies was cooling on the wire rack when the window-cleaners arrived – not a pair of them, as usual, but four, and wanted some milk for their tea, and gazed at the mince-pies like hungry schoolboys until I offered them and they took two each, so I had to start on more pastry. Then a friend from the other side of the village brought a Christmas fruit loaf, and then another neighbour with two small sons and a party invitation arrived and the kettle went on and more pies disappeared. The kitchen was packed with happy people and over the wireless came the first of the Nine Lessons and Carols from King's College, Cambridge.

By the time everyone had left, nearly two dozen of the mince-pies and a lot of sausage rolls had been consumed and there were none for us or the carol singers. I heaved another bag of flour out of the larder.

SUSAN HILL
The Magic Apple Tree 1982

On Christmas Eve a great quantity of holly and of laurel is brought in from the garden and from the farm (for this house has a farm of a hundred acres attached to it and an oak wood of ten acres). This greenery is put up all over the house in every room just before it comes dark on that day. Then there is brought in to the hall a young pine tree, about twice the height of a man, to serve for a Christmas tree, and on this innumerable little candles are fixed, and presents for all the household and the guests and the children of the village.

It is at about five o'clock that these last come into the house, and at that hour in England, at that date, it has long been quite dark; so they come into a house all illuminated with the Christmas tree shining like a cluster of many stars seen through a glass.

The first thing done after the entry of these people from the village and their children (the children are in number about fifty) is a common meal, where all eat and drink their fill in the offices. Then the children come in to the Christmas tree. They are each given a silver piece one by one, and one by one, their presents. After that they dance in the hall and sing songs, which have been handed down to them for I do not know how long. The men and things and animals which you hear mentioned in these songs are all of that countryside. Indeed, the tradition of Christmas here is what it should be everywhere, knit into the very stuff of the place; so that I fancy the little children, when they think of Bethlehem, see it in their minds as though it were in the winter depth of England, which is as it should be.

HILAIRE BELLOC
A Remaining Christmas 1928 (Conversations with an Angel)

Dusk fell at tea-time on Christmas Eve at Thrush Green. There was an air of expectancy everywhere. The windows of St Andrew's church glowed with muted reds and blues against the black bulk of the ancient stones, for inside devoted ladies were putting last minute touches to the altar flowers and the holly wreath around the font.

Paul Young and his friend Christopher lay on their stomachs before the crackling log fire. The sound of carol singing made them both sit up. Breathless, tingling with the anticipation of Christmas joys, they rushed into the hall.

The boys watched entranced as the carol singers formed a tidy crescent round the doorstep. Some held torches, and a tall boy supported a hurricane lamp at the end of a stout hazel pole. It swung gently as he moved and was far more decorative in the winter darkness, as it glowed with a soft amber light, than the more efficient torches of his neighbours.

Joan Young opened the door hospitably, the better to hear the singing, and the choir master tapped his tuning fork against the edge of the door, hummed the note resonantly to his attentive choir, and off they went robustly into the first bars of "It came upon the midnight clear".

Their breath rolled from their tuneful mouths in great silver clouds, wreathing about their heads and the sheets of music clenched in their gloved hands. In the distance the bells of Lulling Church could be faintly heard, as the singers paused for breath.

A dead leaf scurried about the doorstep adding its whispers to the joyful full-throated chorus above it. The bare winter trees in the garden lifted their arms to the stars above, straining, it seemed to young Paul, to reach as high as St Andrew's steeple

The boys gazed enraptured, strangely moved by this manifestation of praise. It seemed to be shared by everything that had life.

MISS READ
Winter in Thrush Green 1961

She hung up her stocking at the foot of the bed and fell asleep. But soon singing roused her, and she sat up, bewildered. Yes, it was the carol-singers.

Outside under the stars she could see the group of men and women with lanterns throwing beams across the paths and on to the stable door. One man stood apart beating time, another played a fiddle, and another had a flute. The rest sang in four parts the Christmas hymns.

There was a star, Susan could see it twinkling and bright in the dark boughs with their white frosted layers, and there was a stable. She watched the faces half lit by the lanterns, top-coats pulled up to their necks. The music of the violin came thin and squeaky, like a singing icicle, blue and cold, but magic, and the flute was warm like the voices.

They stopped and waited a moment. Tom's deep voice came from the darkness. They trooped, chattering and puffing out their cheeks, and clapping their arms round their bodies to the front door. They were going into the parlour for elderberry wine and their collection money. A bright light flickered across the snow as the door was flung wide open. Then a bang, and Susan went back to bed.

Christmas Eve was nearly over, but tomorrow was Christmas Day, the best day in all the year. She shut her eyes and fell asleep.

ALISON UTTLEY
The Country Child 1931

Winifred and Grace, aged four and six-and-a-half, lay awake on Christmas Eve gazing through the square uncurtained window at the frosty constellations of winter stars. The maids clattering in the pantry below them had at last become silent; only the occasional clank of an iron-shod hoof in the horse-pasture broke the stillness of the night – when suddenly came the crunch of feet on the gravel of the drive, the soft flicker of the lantern, and the joyous tumult of a Christmas carol. In a second the two small girls were out of bed, scampering barefoot along the nursery passage, into the best spare bedroom.

Peering between the slats of the venetian blind, they saw the singers with pale faces and long black coats, standing in the moonlight and starlight and lantern-light and lamplight streaming from the drawing-room window on the semi-circular sweep of the gravel. The chill draught blowing through the cold bedroom was sharp as icy water on the children's shivering bodies; they gathered their nightdresses round them and huddled ecstatically together for warmth as the twenty men and boys from the church choir went on singing round the schoolmaster's lantern. "I can close my eyes and see them," Winifred Holtby wrote a quarter of a century later. "I can shut my ears and hear them. It is all there"

VERA BRITTAIN
Testament of Friendship 1953

The minstrels played their Christmas tune
    To-night beneath my cottage eaves;
While, smitten by a lofty moon,
    The encircling laurels, thick with leaves,
Gave back a rich and dazzling sheen
That overpowered their natural green.

Through hill and vale every breeze
    Had sunk to rest with folded wings:
Keen was the air, but could not freeze
    Nor check the music of the strings;
So stout and hardy were the band
That scraped the chords with strenuous hand!

And who but listened – till was paid
    Respect to every inmate's claim:
The greeting given, the music played,
    In honour of each household name,
Duly pronounced with lusty call,
And "Merry Christmas" wished to all!

How touching, when, at midnight, sweep
    Snow-muffled winds, and all is dark,
To hear – and sink again to sleep!
    Or, at an earlier call, to mark,
By blazing fire, the still suspense
Of self-complacent innocence;

WILLIAM WORDSWORTH
Sonnets to the River Duddon 1820

As we approached the house, we heard the sound of music, and now and then a burst of laughter from one end of the building. This, Bracebridge said, must proceed from the servants' hall, where a great deal of revelry was permitted, and even encouraged, by the Squire, throughout the twelve days of Christmas, provided every thing was done conformably to ancient custom. Here were kept up the old games of hoodman blind, shoe the wild mare, hot cockles, steal the white loaf, Bob apple, and snap dragon: the Yule clog, and Christmas candle, were regularly burnt, and the mistletoe, with its white berries, hung up, to the imminent peril of all the pretty housemaids.

While the mutual greetings were going on between young Bracebridge and his relatives, I had time to scan the apartment. I have called it a hall, for so it had certainly been in old times, and the Squire had evidently endeavoured to restore it to something of its primitive state.

The grate had been removed from the wide overwhelming fireplace, to make way for a fire of wood, in the midst of which was an enormous log glowing and blazing, and sending forth a vast volume of light and heat: this I understood was the Yule clog, which the Squire was particular in having brought in and illumined on a Christmas eve, according to ancient custom.

The Yule clog is a great log of wood, sometimes the root of a tree, brought into the house with great ceremony, on Christmas Eve, laid in the fireplace, and lighted with the brand of last year's clog. While it lasted, there was great drinking, singing, and telling of tales. Sometimes it is accompanied by Christmas candles; but in the cottages the only light was from the ruddy blaze of the great wood fire. The Yule clog was to burn all night; if it went out, it was considered a sign of ill luck. The brand remaining from the Yule clog is carefully put away to light the next year's Christmas fire.

It was really delightful to see the old Squire, seated in his hereditary elbow chair, by the hospitable fireside of his ancestors, and looking around him like the sun of a system, beaming warmth and gladness to every heart. Even the very dog that lay stretched at his feet, as he lazily shifted his position and yawned, would look fondly up in his master's face, wag his tail against the floor, and stretch himself again to sleep, confident of kindness and protection. There is an emanation from the heart in genuine hospitality, which cannot be described, but is immediately felt, and puts the stranger at once at his ease.

Supper was announced shortly after our arrival. It was served up in a spacious oaken chamber, the pannels of which shone with wax, and around which were several family portraits decorated with holly and ivy. Besides the accustomed lights, two great wax tapers, called Christmas candles, wreathed with greens, were placed on a highly polished beaufet among the family plate. The table was abundantly spread with substantial fare; but the Squire made his supper of frumenty, a dish made of wheat cakes, boiled in milk with rich spices; being a standing dish in old times, for Christmas eve. I was happy to find my old friend, minced pie, in the retinue of the feast, and finding him to be perfectly orthodox, and that I need not be ashamed of my predilection, I greeted him with all the warmth wherewith we usually greet an old and very genteel acquaintance.

WASHINGTON IRVING
Sketch Book 1820

What might be called the dining-room part, though rich, was rather sombre on ordinary occasions; but this night it was decorated gloriously. The materials were simple wax-candles and holly; the effect was produced by a magnificent use of these materials. There were eighty candles of the largest size sold in shops, and twelve wax pillars, five feet high, and the size of a man's calf; of these, four only were lighted at present. The holly was not in sprigs, but in enormous branches, that filled the eye with glistening green and red; and in the embrasure of the front window stood a young holly-tree entire, eighteen feet high, and gorgeous with five hundred branches of red berries. The tree had been dug up, and planted here in an enormous bucket, used for that purpose, and filled with mould. Close behind this tree were placed two of the wax pillars, lighted, and their flame shone through the leaves and berries magically.

The schoolchildren and young people of the village trooped in and made their obeisances, and sang the Christmas Carol. Then one of the party produced an image of the Virgin and Child, and another offered comfits in a box; a third presented the wassail cup, into which Raby immediately poured some silver.

The wassailers departed, and the Squire went to say a kind word to his humbler guests.....

It was nearly eleven o'clock when Mr Raby rejoined them, and they all went in to supper. There were candles lighted on the table and a few here and there upon the walls; but the room was very sombre; and Mr Raby informed them that this was to remind them of the moral darkness in which the world lay before that great event they were about to celebrate.

He then helped each of them to a ladleful of frumenty, remarking at the same time, with a grim smile, that they were not obliged to eat it; there would be a very different supper after midnight.

Then a black-letter Bible was brought to him, and he read it all to himself at a side table.

After an interval of silence so passed, there was a gentle tap at the bay window. Mr Raby went and threw it open, and immediately a woman's voice, clear and ringing, sang outside – "The first Noel the angels did say…."

As the Noel proceeded, some came in at the window, others at the doors, and the lower part of the room began to fill with singers and auditors.

CHARLES READE
Put Yourself in His Place 1874

"Yo ho, my boys!" said Fezziwig. "No more work to-night. Christmas Eve, Dick. Christmas, Ebenezer! Let's have the shutters up," cried old Fezziwig, with a sharp clap of his hands, "before a man can say Jack Robinson!"

You wouldn't believe how those two fellows went at it! They charged into the street with the shutters – one, two, three – had 'em up in their places – four, five, six – barred 'em and pinned 'em – seven, eight, nine – and came back before you could have got to twelve, panting like race-horses.

"Hilli-ho!" cried old Fezziwig, skipping down from the high desk, with wonderful agility. "Clear away, my lads, and let's have lots of room here! Hilli-ho, Dick! Chirrup, Ebenezer!"

Clear away! There was nothing they wouldn't have cleared away, or couldn't have cleared away, with old Fezziwig looking on. It was done in a minute. Every movable was packed off, as if it were dismissed from public life for evermore; the floor was swept and watered, the lamps were trimmed, fuel was heaped upon the fire; and the warehouse was as snug, and warm, and dry, and bright a ball-room, as you would desire to see upon a winter's night.

In came a fiddler with a music-book, and went up to the lofty desk, and made an orchestra of it, and tuned like fifty stomach-aches. In came Mrs Fezziwig, one vast substantial smile. In came the three Miss Fezziwigs, beaming and lovable. In came the six young followers whose hearts they broke. In came all the young men and women employed in the business. In came the housemaid, with her cousin, the baker. In came the cook, with her brother's particular friend, the milkman. In came the boy from over the way, who was suspected of not having board enough from his master; trying to hide himself behind the girl from next door but one, who proved to have had her ears pulled by her mistress. In they all came, one after another; some shyly, some boldly, some gracefully, some awkwardly, some pushing, some pulling; in they all came, anyhow and everyhow. Away they all went, twenty couple at once; hands half round and back again the other way; down the middle and up again; round and round in various stages of affectionate grouping; old top couple always turning up in the wrong place; new top couple starting off again, as soon as they got there; all top couples at last, and not a bottom one to help them! When this result was brought about, old Fezziwig, clapping his hands to stop the dance, cried out, "Well done!" and the fiddler plunged his hot face into a pot of porter, especially provided for that purpose. But scorning rest, upon his reappearance, he instantly began again, though there were no dancers yet, as if the other fiddler had been carried home, exhausted, on a shutter, and he were a bran-new man resolved to beat him out of sight, or perish.

There were more dances, and there were forfeits, and more dances, and there was cake, and there was negus, and there was a great piece of Cold Roast, and there was a great piece of Cold Boiled, and there were mince-pies, and plenty of beer. But the great effect of the evening came after the Roast and Boiled, when the fiddler (an artful dog, mind! The sort of man who knew his business better than you or I could have told it him!) struck up "Sir Roger de Coverley." Then old Fezziwig stood out to dance with Mrs Fezziwig. Top couple, too; with a good stiff piece of work cut out for them; three or four and twenty pair of partners; people who were not to be trifled with; people who *would* dance, and had no notion of walking.

But if there had been twice as many – ah, four times – old Fezziwig would have been a match for them, and so would Mrs Fezziwig. As to *her*, she was worthy to be his partner in every sense of the term. If that's not high praise, tell me higher, and I'll use it. A positive light appeared to issue from Fezziwig's calves. They shone in every part of the dance like moons. You couldn't have predicted, at any given time, what would have become of them next. And when old Fezziwig and Mrs Fezziwig had gone all through the dance; advance and retire, both hands to your partner, bow and curtsey, corkscrew, thread-the-needle, and back again to your place; Fezziwig "cut" – cut so deftly, that he appeared to wink with his legs, and came upon his feet again without a stagger.

When the clock struck eleven, this domestic ball broke up. Mr and Mrs Fezziwig took their stations, one on either side of the door, and shaking hands with every person individually as he or she went out, wished him or her a Merry Christmas. When everybody had retired but the two 'prentices, they did the same to them; and thus the cheerful voices died away, and the lads were left to their beds; which were under a counter in the back shop.

CHARLES DICKENS
A Christmas Carol 1843

From the centre of the ceiling of this kitchen, old Wardle had just suspended, with his own hands, a huge branch of mistletoe, and this same branch of mistletoe instantaneously gave rise to a scene of general and delightful struggling and confusion; in the midst of which, Mr Pickwick, with a gallantry that would have done honour to a descendant of Lady Tollimglower herself, took the old lady by the hand, led her beneath the mystic branch, and saluted her in all courtesy and decorum. The old lady submitted to this piece of practical politeness with all the dignity which befitted so important and serious a solemnity, but the younger ladies, not being so thoroughly imbued with a superstitious veneration for the custom: or imagining that the value of a salute is very much enhanced if it cost a little trouble to obtain it: screamed and struggled, and ran into corners, and threatened and remonstrated, and did everything but leave the room, until some of the less adventurous gentlemen were on the point of desisting, when they all at once found it useless to resist any longer, and submitted to be kissed with good grace. Mr Winkle kissed the young lady with the black eyes, and Mr Snodgrass kissed Emily, and Mr Weller, not being particular about the form of being under the mistletoe, kissed Emma and the other female servants, just as he caught them. As to the poor relations, they kissed everybody, not even excepting the plainer portions of the young-lady visitors, who, in their excessive confusion, ran right under the mistletoe, as soon as it was hung up, without knowing it! Wardle stood with his back to the fire, surveying the whole scene, with the utmost satisfaction; and the fat boy took the opportunity of appropriating to his own use, and summarily devouring, a particularly fine mince-pie, that had been carefully put by for somebody else.

Now, the screaming had subsided, and faces were in a glow, and curls in a tangle, and Mr Pickwick, after kissing the old lady as before mentioned, was standing under the mistletoe, looking with a very pleased countenance on all that was passing around him, when the young lady with the black eyes, after a little whispering with the other young ladies, made a sudden dart forward, and, putting her arm round Mr Pickwick's neck, saluted him affectionately on the left cheek; and before Mr Pickwick distinctly knew what was the matter, he was surrounded by the whole body, and kissed by every one of them.

It was a pleasant thing to see Mr Pickwick in the centre of the group, now pulled this way, and then that, and first kissed on the chin, and then on the nose, and then on the spectacles: and to hear the peals of laughter which were raised on every side; but it was a still more pleasant thing to see Mr Pickwick, blinded shortly afterwards with a silk handkerchief, falling up against the wall, and scrambling into corners, and going through all the mysteries of blind-man's buff, with the utmost relish for the game, until at last he caught one of the poor relations, and then had to evade the blind-man himself, which he did with a nimbleness and agility that elicited the admiration and applause of all beholders. The poor relations caught just the people who they thought would like it, and when the game flagged, got caught themselves. When they were all tired of blind-man's buff, there was a great game at snap-dragon, and when fingers enough were burned with that, and all the raisins were gone, they sat down by the huge fire of blazing logs to a substantial supper, and a mighty bowl of wassail, something smaller than an ordinary wash-house copper, in which the hot apples were hissing and bubbling with a rich look, and a jolly sound, that were perfectly irresistible.

"This," said Mr Pickwick, looking round him, "this is, indeed, comfort."

"Our invariable custom," replied Mr Wardle. "Everybody sits down with us on Christmas Eve, as you see them now – servants and all; and here we wait till the clock strikes twelve, to usher Christmas in, and while away the time with forfeits and old stories. Trundle, my boy, rake up the fire."

Up flew the bright sparks in myriads as the logs were stirred, and the deep red blaze sent forth a rich glow, that penetrated into the farthest corner of the room, and cast its cheerful tint on every face.

CHARLES DICKENS
The Pickwick Papers 1837

The servants had a dance. That was the most extraordinary thing, because they used to dance in the courtyard and that's open to the elements – why they weren't all frozen to death I don't know – and a band used to come down and play and if it was snowing, it was just bad luck. Again, on Christmas Eve we had another dance in the dining room for the sort of upper strata of servants; the housekeepers, the house steward, the butler, the head cook, and all that sort of thing. My mother used to dance with the house steward and my father with the housekeeper to start the thing going, and I think on the whole they had a good time.

6th MARQUIS OF BATH
Pre 1914
(Christmas Past, Gavin Weightman and Steve Humphries)

The supper had disposed everyone to gayety, and an old harper was summoned from the servants' hall, where he had been strumming all the evening, and to all appearance comforting himself with some of the Squire's home brewed.

The dance, like most dances after supper, was a merry one: some of the older folks joined in it, and the Squire himself figured down several couple with a partner with whom he affirmed he had danced at every Christmas for nearly half a century.

The party now broke up for the night with the kind hearted old custom of shaking hands. As I passed through the hall, on my way to my chamber, the dying embers of the Yule clog still sent forth a dusky glow, and had it not been the season when "no spirit dares stir abroad," I should have been half tempted to steal from my room at midnight, and peep, whether the fairies might not be at their revels.

WASHINGTON IRVING
Sketch Book 1820

The moment Scrooge's hand was on the lock, a strange voice called him by his name, and bade him enter. He obeyed.

It was his own room. There was no doubt about that. But it had undergone a surprising transformation. The walls and ceiling were so hung with living green, that it looked a perfect grove; from every part of which, bright gleaming berries glistened. The crisp leaves of holly, mistletoe, and ivy reflected back the light, as if so many little mirrors had been scattered there; and such a mighty blaze went roaring up the chimney, as that dull petrification of a hearth had never known in Scrooge's time, or Marley's, or for many and many a winter season gone. Heaped up on the floor, to form a kind of throne, were turkeys, geese, game, poultry, brawn, great joints of meat, sucking-pigs, long wreaths of sausages, mince-pies, plum-puddings, barrels of oysters, red-hot chestnuts, cherry-cheeked apples, juicy oranges, luscious pears, immense twelfth-cakes, and seething bowls of punch, that made the chamber dim with their delicious steam.

CHARLES DICKENS
A Christmas Carol 1843

Sir Roger, after the laudable custom of his ancestors, always keeps open house at Christmas. I learned from him, that he had killed eight fat hogs for this season, that he had dealt about his chines very liberally amongst his neighbours, and that in particular he had sent a string of hog's puddings with a pack of cards to every poor family in the parish. "I have often thought," says Sir Roger, "it happens very well that Christmas should fall out in the middle of the winter. It is the most dead, uncomfortable time of the year, when the poor people would suffer very much from their poverty and cold, if they had not good cheer, warm fires, and Christmas gambols to support them. I love to rejoice their poor hearts at this season, and to see the whole village merry in my great hall. I allow a double quantity of malt to my small beer, and set it a running a Twelve Days for every one that calls for it. I have always a piece of cold beef and a mincepie upon the table, and am wonderfully pleased to see my tenants pass away a whole evening in playing their innocent tricks, and smutting one another."

JOSEPH ADDISON
The Spectator Circa 1700

On Christmas eve the bells were rung
On Christmas eve the mass was sung:
That only night in all the year,
Saw the stoled priest the chalice rear.
The damsel donn'd her kirtle sheen;
The hall was dressed with holly green;
Forth to the wood did merry-men go,
To gather in the mistletoe.
Then open'd wide the Baron's hall
To vassal, tenant, serf, and all;
Power laid his rod of rule aside,
And Ceremony doff'd his pride.
The heir with roses in his shoes,
That night might village partner choose.
The Lord, underogating, share
The vulgar game of "post and pair".
All hail'd, with uncontroll'd delight,
And general voice, the happy night,
That to the cottage, as the crown,
Brought tidings of salvation down.
The fire, with well-dried logs supplied,
Went roaring up the chimney wide;
The huge hall-table's oaken face,
Scrubb'd till it shone, the day to grace,
Bore then upon its massive board
No mark to part the squire and lord.
Then was brought in the lusty brawn,
By old blue-coated serving-man;
Then the grim boar's head frown'd on high,
Crested with bays and rosemary.
Well can the green-garb'd ranger tell,
How, when, and where, the monster fell;
What dogs before his death he tore,

And all the baiting of the boar.
The wassel round, in good brown bowls,
Garnish'd with ribbons, blithely trowels.
There the huge sirloin reek'd; hard by
Plumb-porridge stood, and Christmas pie;
Or fail'd old Scotland to produce,
At such high tide, her savoury goose.
Then came the merry maskers in,
And carols roar'd with blithesome din;
If unmelodious was the song,
It was a hearty note, and strong.
Who lists may in their mumming see
Traces of ancient mystery;
White shirts supplied the masquerade,
And smutted cheeks the visors made;
But, O! what maskers, richly dight,
Can boast of bosoms half so light!
England was merry England, when
Old Christmas brought his sports again.
'Twas Christmas broach'd the mightiest ale;
'Twas Christmas told the merriest tale;
A Christmas gambol oft could cheer
The poor man's heart through all the year.

SIR WALTER SCOTT
Marmion 1808

It was Christmas Eve on a Friday,
The shops was full of cheer,
With tinsel in the windows,
And presents twice as dear.
A thousand Father Christmases
Sat in their little huts,
And folk was buying crackers
And folk was buying nuts.

All up and down the country,
Before the light was snuffed,
Turkeys they got murdered,
And cockerels they got stuffed.
Christmas cakes got marzipanned,
And puddins they got steamed,
Mothers they got desperate,
And tired kiddies screamed.

Hundredweights of Christmas cards
Went flying through the post,
With first-class stamps on those
You had to flatter most.
Within a million kitchens,
Mince pies was being made,
On everybody's radio,
"White Christmas" it was played.

Out in the frozen countryside,
Men crept round on their own,
Hacking off the holly
What other folks had grown.
Mistletoe in willow trees
Was by a man wrenched clear,
So he could kiss his neighbour's wife
He'd fancied all the year.

And out upon the hillside
Where the Christmas trees had stood,
All was completely barren
But for little stumps of wood.
The little trees that flourished
All the year were there no more,
But in a million houses
Dropped their needles on the floor.

And out of every cranny, cupboard,
Hiding place and nook,
Little bikes and kiddies' trikes
Were secretively took.
Yards of wrapping paper
Was rustled round about,
And bikes were wheeled to bedrooms
With the pedals sticking out.

Rolled up in Christmas paper,
The Action Men were tensed,
All ready for the morning,
When their fighting life commenced.
With tommy guns and daggers,
All clustered round about,
"Peace on Earth - Goodwill to Men",
The figures seemed to shout.

The church was standing empty,
The pub was standing packed,
There came a yell, "Noel, Noel!"
And glasses they got cracked.
From up above the fireplace,
Christmas cards began to fall,
And trodden on the floor, said:
"Merry Xmas, to you all."

PAM AYRES
Goodwill to Men : Give us your Money 1992

8
Getting Ready for Santa

Dear Editor,
I am eight years old. Some of my little friends say there is no Santa Claus. Please tell me the truth, is there a Santa Claus?

VIRGINIA O'HANLON

Dear Virginia,
Your little friends are wrong. They do not believe except they see. They think that nothing can be, which is not comprehensible by their little minds. Yes, there is a Santa Claus. He exists as certainly as love and generosity and devotion exist, and you know that they exist and give to your life its highest beauty and joy. Alas! How dreary the world would be if there was no Santa Claus. There would be no childlike faith then, no poetry, no romance to make tolerable this existence. We should have no enjoyment, except in sense and sight. The eternal light with which childhood fills the world would be extinguished.

Not believe in Santa Claus! Thank God he lives, and he lives forever. A thousand years from now, Virginia, nay ten times ten thousand years from now, he will continue to make glad the heart of childhood.

New York Sun 1897

Then they all sat down round the fire to write their wishes on bits of paper, and see whether they would burn, or fly up the chimney. If they did the latter, it was a sign that Santa Claus had them safe, and would bring the things wished for.

When they had written these lists they threw them into the fire. The fire gave a flicker just then, and the papers vanished. Nobody saw exactly how. John thought they flew up the chimney, but Dorry said they didn't.

Phil dropped his piece in very solemnly. It flamed for a minute, then sank into ashes.

"There, you won't get it, whatever it was!" said Dorry.

And now Clover produced her list. She dropped it into the fire and behold, it flew straight up the chimney.

"How queer!" said Katy; "none of the rest of them did that."

The truth was, that Clover, who was a canny little mortal, had slipped across the room and opened the door just before putting her wishes in. This, of course, made a draught, and sent the paper right upwards.

SUSAN COOLIDGE
What Katy Did 1911

As we were going to sit up for late dinner on Christmas night, we were packed off to bed early. I did not mind this, as it was good to lie in bed and contemplate the morrow. I could hear the sound of church bells and the distant shoutings of the poulterer as he sold off his turkeys. Cyril and I had hung our stockings at the foot of the bed, and I tried to keep awake to see what happened in the night, but my effort was of no avail.

ERNEST H. SHEPARD
Drawn from Memory 1957

On Christmas Eve I hung at the foot of my bed Bessie Bunter's black stocking, and always, I said, I would stay awake all the moonlit, snowlit night to hear the roof-alighting reindeer and see the hollied boot descend through soot. But soon the sand of the snow drifted into my eyes, and, though I stared towards the fireplace and around the flickering room, where the black sack-like stocking hung, I was asleep before the chimney trembled and the room was red and white with Christmas.

DYLAN THOMAS
Conversation about Christmas (1914-1953)

Every Christmas Eve we would hang up our stockings over a large fire in the kitchen, and then mummy would place a chair for Father Christmas to sit on, because he had worked hard. Then we'd put out a plate with a mince pie, and a piece of Christmas cake, and a glass of wine for his refreshment. In the morning, there would be a few crumbs left on the plate, and a big black thumb mark, so we knew Santa Claus had been.

JOAN PRINGLE
Between the wars
(Christmas Past, Gavin Weightman and Steve Humphries)

"Tonight is Christmas Eve, my dears," said Mother blithe and hearty.
"Tomorrow will be Christmas Day and we shall have a party.
So go and hang your stockings up and then they will be ready,
If Santa Claus should bring a toy for Grace and Tom and Teddy."

Then little Grace looked up at her and said in tones appealing,
"I wonder if Santa Claus can tell how little girls are feeling.
I've longed and longed for such a time, to have a dear new dolly.
I haven't got one now to love, except poor broken Molly.

If only he would bring me one with hair so soft and curly,
So I could find her when I wake up so very, very early.
I'd dress her in that pretty frock, you made me for my other
And love dear Santa, oh so much, almost as much as Mother."

Said little Ted, "I'm five years old, a box of bricks I'd rather.
I'm much too old for babies' toys; I want to build like Father.
Some tools I someday hope to have, to make things, when they let me,
But this year, I just want some bricks. I hope he won't forget me."

Said greedy Tom, "I would not ask for just one thing, but twenty.
Old Santa Claus has heaps of toys, I'm sure he'll bring me plenty;
A whip, a kite, a humming top, a ball, a clown so funny,
A car, a ship, an aeroplane, also a purse of money."

The morning came; Grace found her doll, with hair so soft and pretty,
And Ted a lovely box of bricks, enough to build a city.
But greedy Tom his stocking seized, so eager to begin it.
Although he searched from top to toe, he found just nothing in it.

(Poor Tom went down to breakfast late and found a present on his plate.)

ANON.

9
The Evening Service

Every year, at half-past five on Christmas Eve, Michael lifted his great fist and struck the double quarter, and the Cathedral bells rang out. They pealed for half-an-hour and all over the city, and in all the villages to which the wind carried the sound of the bells, they knew that Christmas had begun. People in the fen wrapped cloaks about them and went out of doors and stood looking towards the city. This year it was bitterly cold but the wind had swept the clouds away and the Cathedral on its hill towered up among the stars, light shining from its windows. Below it the twinkling city lights were like clustering fireflies about its feet. The tremendous bell music that was rocking the tower and pealing through the city was out here as lovely and far away as though it rang out from the stars themselves, and it caught at men's hearts. "Now 'tis Christmas," they said to each other, as their forebears had said for centuries past, looking towards the city on the hill and the great fane that was as much a part of their blood and bones as the fen itself. " 'Tis Christmas," they said, and went back happy to their homes.

In the city, as soon as the bells started, everyone began to get ready. Then from nearly every house family parties came out and made their way up the steep streets towards the Cathedral. Quite small children were allowed to stay up for the carol service, and they chattered like sparrows as they stumped along buttoned into their thick coats, the boys gaitered and mufflered, the girls with muffs and fur bonnets. It was the custom in the city to put lighted candles in the windows on Christmas Eve and their light, and the light of the street lamps, made of the street ladders of light leaning against the hill. The grown-ups found them Jacob's ladders to-night, easy to climb, for the bells and the children tugged them up.

Some of them only came to the Cathedral on this one day in the year, but as they entered the nave they felt the impact of its beauty no less keenly than those who came often. It was always like a blow between the eyes, but especially at night, and especially on Christmas Eve when they were full of awe and expectation.

The great pillars soared into darkness and the aisles narrowed to twilight. Candles twinkled in the choir and the high altar with its flowers was ablaze with them, but all the myriad flames were no more than seed pearls embroidered on a dark cloak. The great rood was veiled in shadow. All things alike went out into mystery. The crowd of tiny human creatures flowed up the nave and on to the benches. The sound of their feet, of their whispering voices and rustling garments, was lost in the vastness. The music of the organ flowed over them and they were still.

Then it stopped, and the bells too, and there was silence, and then miles away he heard boys singing. They came nearer and nearer, singing like the birds out in the fen in spring. One by one men's voices began to join in, and then the multitude of men and women whom he could scarcely see began to sing too. The sound grew, soaring up to the great darkness overhead. It pulled him to his feet. He dared not use his coarsened voice but the music sang in his blood like sap rising in a tree. When the hymn ended there was a strange rustling sound, like leaves stirring all over a vast forest. It startled him at first until he realised that it was all the toffs kneeling down. He knelt too, his tattered cap in his hands.

There was silence again and far away he heard the Dean's voice raised in the bidding prayer. He could not distinguish a word but the familiar voice banished the last of his fear. When the prayer ended he said Amen as loudly as any and was no longer conscious of the loneliness. From then until the end he was hardly conscious even of himself. There were not many who were. They were not to-night on the normal plane of human experience. When they had climbed the Jacob's ladders of the lighted streets from the city to the Cathedral they had climbed up just one rung higher than they usually did.

ELIZABETH GOUDGE
The Dean's Watch 1960

They arrived just as the Mass was beginning. There were crowds of people and no chance of getting a seat. The aisles were lit by naked electric globes and they threw harsh beams on the vaulting, the columns and the dark throng of worshippers. The choir was brilliantly lit. There was an orchestra on a raised platform. At the altar were priests in splendid vestments. The music seemed to Charley somewhat florid and he had a feeling that he was listening to a performance rather than attending a religious ceremony, and it excited in him no sensation of reverence. But for all that, he was glad to have come. The darkness into which the light from the electric globes cut like a bright knife, making the Gothic lines grimmer; the soft brilliance of the altar, with its multitude of candles, with the priests performing actions whose meaning was unknown to him; the silent crowd that seemed not to participate but to wait anxiously like a crowd at a station barrier waiting for the gate to open; the stench of wet clothes and the aromatic perfume of incense; the bitter cold that lowered like a threatening unseen presence; it was not a religious emotion that he got from all this, but the sense of a mystery that had its roots far back in the origins of the human race. His nerves were taut, and when of a sudden the choir to the full accompaniment of the orchestra burst with a great shout into the Adeste Fidelis he was seized with an exultation over he knew not what. Then a boy sang a canticle; the thin, silvery voice rose in the silence and the notes trickled, with a curious hesitation at first, as though the singer were not quite sure of himself; and then, the singer gathering assurance, the sounds were caught up, as though by great dark hands, and borne into the intricate curves of the arches and up to the night of the vaulted roof.

W. SOMERSET MAUGHAM
Christmas Holiday 1939

69

10
The World Waits – Dawn Breaks

Darkness thickened over Lulling and Thrush Green. The Christmas tree twinkled and blazed in the market square dwarfing the stars above to insignificance.

Excited children for once went willingly to bed, stockings clutched in their rapacious hands and heads whirling with delirious thoughts of joys to come. Exhausted shop assistants sat at home soaking their aching feet in warm water. Housewives, flopping wearily in armchairs, congratulated themselves upon remembering the decorations for the trifle, the cherry sticks for the drinks and other last minute details until they were brought up short by the horrid thought that in the pressure of so much unaccustomed shopping they had completely forgotten salt and tea, and now it was too late anyway.

But away from the lights and worries of the town the quiet hills lay beneath a velvety sky. No wind rustled the trees and no bird disturbed the night's tranquillity. Sheep still roamed the slopes as they had that memorable night so long ago in Palestine, and low on the horizon a great star, bright as a jewel, still held out an eternal promise to mankind.

MISS READ
Winter in Thrush Green 1961

The time draws near the birth of Christ;
The moon is hid – the night is still;
The Christmas bells from hill to hill
Answer each other in the mist.

Rise, happy morn! Rise, holy morn!
Draw forth the cheerful day from night;
O Father touch the east, and light
The light that shone when hope was born!

ALFRED LORD TENNYSON
The Birth of Christ 1833 (In Memoriam)
70

The expectation grew more tense. The star was risen into the sky, the songs, the carols were ready to hail it. The star was the sign in the sky. Earth too should give a sign. As evening drew on, hearts beat fast with anticipation, hands were full of ready gifts. There were the tremulously expectant words of the church service, the night was past and the morning was come, the gifts were given and received, joy and peace made a flapping of wings in each heart, there was a great burst of carols, the Peace of the World had dawned, strife had passed away, every hand was linked in hand, every heart was singing.

D.H. LAWRENCE
The Rainbow 1915

Christmass is come and every hearth
Makes room to give him welcome now
E'en want will dry its tears in mirth
And crown him wi' a holly bough
Tho' tramping 'neath a winter's sky
O'er snowy track paths and ryhmey stiles
The huswife sets her spining bye
And bids him welcome wi' her smiles.

Each house is swept the day before
And windows stuck wi' evergreens
The snow is beesom'd from the door
And comfort crowns the cottage scenes
Gilt holly wi' its thorny pricks
And yew and box wi' berrys small
These deck the unus'd candlesticks
And pictures hanging by the wall.

Neighbours resume their annual cheer
Wishing wi' smiles and spirits high
Glad Christmass and a happy year
To every morning passer-by
Milk maids their Christmass journeys go
Accompanyd wi' favour'd swain
And childern pace the crumping snow
To taste their granny's cake again.

Hung wi' the ivys veining bough
The ash trees round the cottage farm
Are often stript of branches now
The cotter's Christmass hearth to warm
He swings and twists his hazel band
And lops them off wi' sharpened hook
And oft brings ivy in his hand
To decorate the chimney nook.

Old winter whipes his icicles bye
And warms his fingers till he smiles
Where cottage hearths are blazing high
And labour resteth from his toils
Wi' merry mirth beguiling care
Old customs keeping wi' the day
Friends meet their Christmass cheer to share
And pass it in a harmless way.

Old customs O I love the sound
However simple they may be
What ere with time has sanction found
Is welcome and is dear to me
Pride grows above simplicity
And spurns it from her haughty mind
And soon the poets song will be
The only refuge they can find.

The shepherd now no more afraid
Since custom doth the chance bestow
Starts up to kiss the giggling maid
Beneath the branch of mizzletoe
That 'neath each cottage beam is seen
Wi' pearl-like berrys shining gay
The shadow still of what hath been
Which fashion yearly fades away.

And singers too a merry throng
At early morn wi' simple skill
Yet imitate the angels' song
And chant their Christmass ditty still

And mid the storm that dies and swells
By fits-in humings softly steals
The music of the village bells
Ringing round their merry peals.

And when it's past a merry crew
Bedeckt in masks and ribbons gay
The "Morrice danse" their sports renew
And act their winter evening play
The clown-turnd-kings for penny praise
Storm wi' the actors strut and swell
And harlequin a laugh to raise
Wears his hump back and tinkling bell.

And oft for pence and spicy ale
Wi' winter nosegays pind before
The wassail singer tells her tale
And drawls her Christmass carrols o'er
The prentice boy wi' ruddy face
And rhyme bepowder'd dancing locks
From door to door wi' happy pace
Runs round to claim his "Christmass box".

The block behind the fire is put
To sanction customs old desires
And many a faggots bands are cut
For the old farmers Christmass fires
Where loud tong'd gladness joins the throng
And winter meets the warmth of May
Feeling by times the heat too strong
And rubs his shins and draws away.

While snow the window panes bedim
The fire curls up a sunny charm
Where creaming o'er the pitchers rim
The flowering ale is set to warm
Mirth full of joy as summer bees
Sits there its pleasures to impart
While childern 'tween their parents knees
Sing scraps of carrols o'er by heart.

And some to view the winter weathers
Climb up the window seat wi' glee
Likening the snow to falling feathers
In fancy's infant extacy
Laughing wi' superstitious love
O'er visions wild that youth supplyes
Of people pulling geese above
And keeping Christmass in the skyes.

As tho' homestead trees were drest
In lieu of snow wi' dancing leaves
As tho' the sundryd martin's nest
Instead of icicles hung the eaves
The children hail the happy day
As if the snow was April grass
And pleased as 'neath the warmth of May
Sport o'er the water froze to glass.

Thou day of happy sound and mirth
That long wi' childish memory stays
How blest around the cottage hearth
I met thee in my boyish days
Harping wi' raptures dreaming joys
On presents that thy coming found
The welcome sight of little toys
The Christmass gifts of comers round.

The wooden horse wi' arching head
Drawn upon wheels around the room
The gilded coach of ginger bread
And many color'd sugar plumb
Gilt cover'd books for pictures sought
Or storys childhood loves to tell
Wi' many an urgent promise bought
To get tomorrows lesson well.

Around the glowing hearth at night
The harmless laugh and winter tale
Goes round while parting friends delight
To toast each other o'er their ale

The cotter oft wi' quiet zeal
Will musing o'er his Bible lean
While in the dark the lovers steal
To kiss and toy behind the screen.

The Yule cake dotted thick wi' plumbs
Is on each supper table found
And cats look up for falling crumbs
Which greedy children litter round
And huswifes sage stuff'd season'd chine
Long hung in chimney nook to drye
And boiling eldern berry wine
To drink the Christmas Eve's "good bye".

JOHN CLARE
The Shepherd's Calendar 1827

The Noel ended, there was a silence, during which the organ was opened, the bellows blown, and a number of servants and others came into the room with little lighted tapers, and stood in a long row, awaiting a signal from the Squire.

He took out his watch and, finding it was close on twelve o'clock, directed the doors to be flung open, that he might hear the great clock in the hall strike the quarters.

The clock struck the first quarter – dead silence; the second – the third – dead silence. But at the fourth, and with the first stroke of midnight, out burst the full organ and fifty voices, with the *"Gloria in excelsis Deo"*; and, as that divine hymn surged on, the lighters ran along the walls and lighted the eighty candles, and, for the first time, the twelve waxen pillars, so that, as the hymn concluded, the room was in a blaze, and it was Christmas Day.

CHARLES READE
Put Yourself in His Place 1874

Oh, glorious! Glorious! Christmas Day.

CHARLES DICKENS
A Christmas Carol 1843

This is Christmas Day, it's Christmas Day, it won't come again for a whole year. It's Christmas.

ALISON UTTLEY
The Country Child 1931

The combined churches' choir toured the village on several nights... the village band, descended from the church musicians evicted when an organ was installed well over a hundred-and-fifty years ago, called here and elsewhere on Christmas Eve with our favourite carol; it then serenaded the village, starting at 4 a.m. this morning with "Christians Awake" and continuing until the church bells rang out at 7 a.m.

ANDREW SEWELL
Diary 1892

I heard the bells on Christmas Day
Their old familiar carols play,
And wild and sweet
The words repeat
Of peace on earth, good will to men.

And thought how, as the day had come,
The belfries of all Christendom
Had rolled along
The unbroken song
Of peace on earth, good will to men.

Till, singing, on its way
The world revolved from night to day,
A voice, a chime,
A chant sublime
Of peace on earth, good will to men.

HENRY WADSWORTH LONGFELLOW
Christmas Bells 1864

Music I love - - but never strain
Could kindle raptures so divine,
So grief assuage, so conquer pain,
And rouse this pensive heart of mine - -
As that we hear on Christmas morn,
Upon the wintry breezes born.

Though darkness still her empire keep,
And hours must pass, ere morning break;
From troubled dreams, or slumbers deep,
That music kindly bids us wake:
It calls us with an angel's voice,
To wake, and worship, and rejoice.

ANNE BRONTË
Music on Christmas Morning 1843

As I lay awake praying in the early morning I thought I heard a sound of distant bells. It was an intense frost. The morning was most brilliant. Walked to the Sunday School and the road sparkled with millions of rainbows, the seven colours gleaming in every glittering point of hoar frost. The church was very cold in spite of two roaring stove fires.

REV. FRANCIS KILVERT
Diary 1870

Fine old Christmas, with the snowy hair and ruddy face, had done his duty that year in the noblest fashion, and had set off his rich gifts of warmth and colour with all the heightening contrast of frost and snow.

Snow lay on the croft and river-bank in undulations softer than the limbs of infancy; it lay with the neatliest finished border on every sloping roof, making the dark-red gables stand out with a new depth of colour; it weighed heavily on the laurels and fir-trees till it fell from them with a shuddering sound; it clothed the rough turnip field with whiteness, and made the sheep look like dark blotches; the gates were all blocked up with the sloping drifts, and here and there a disregarded four-footed beast stood as if petrified "in unrecumbent sadness"; there was no gleam, no shadow, for the heavens, too, were one still, pale cloud – no sound or motion in anything but the dark river, that flowed and moaned like an unresting sorrow. But old Christmas smiled as he laid this cruel-seeming spell on the out-door world, for he meant to light up home with new brightness, to

77

deepen all the richness of indoor colour, and give a keener edge of delight to the warm fragrance of food: he meant to prepare a sweet imprisonment that would strengthen the primitive fellowship of kindred, and make the sunshine of familiar human faces as welcome as the hidden day-star.

The red berries were just as abundant on the holly, and Maggie had dressed all the windows and mantelpieces and picture-frames on Christmas eve with as much taste as ever, wedding the thick-set scarlet clusters with branches of the black-berried ivy. There had been singing under the windows after midnight – supernatural singing. But the midnight chant had helped as usual to lift the morning above the level of common days; and then there was the smell of hot toast and ale from the kitchen, at the breakfast hour; the favourite anthem, the green boughs, and the short sermon, gave the appropriate festal character to the church-going. The plum-pudding was of the same handsome roundness as ever, and came in with the symbolic blue flames around it. The dessert was as splendid as ever, with its golden oranges, brown nuts, and the crystalline light and dark of apple jelly and damson cheese: in all these things Christmas was as it had always been since Tom could remember.

GEORGE ELIOT
Mill on the Floss 1860

11
Presents

Waking up on Christmas morning in childhood is something that can never be forgotten. First I was conscious of something different about the day, then I remembered, and crawled to the bottom of the bed. It was all right! The stocking was full! I fumbled in the dark and turned out one thing after another. Some were done up in paper. There were crackers and an orange, and an exciting hard box which promised chocolates. I called to Cyril and found he too was exploring in the dark. Then he boldly got out of bed and lit the gas, standing on a chair. This was not allowed, but we felt that on Christmas morning it was different. We laid all our gifts on the bed and opened the chocolates.

ERNEST H. SHEPARD
Drawn from Memory 1957

Colette, being the youngest of the family, was naturally the first to wake up on Christmas morning. She wriggled up from the bottom of her bed and popped her head out. It was still dark, but a faint greying where the window was gave promise of dawn. It was very cold, and Colette, like a tortoise thinking better of it, withdrew her head and crept beneath her shell again. There in the warm darkness she remembered her stocking. She scrambled down to the bottom of the bed, dragged away the bedclothes, thrust her head out of the aperture and grabbed it. Then she retired under cover again, hugging its delicious hard bulkiness to her bosom. She did not want to wake Peronelle by demanding a light, so, having satisfied herself by pinching that the sugar pig was there, and the orange and the apple, and the boiled sweets, and the doll, she fell asleep again, clasping it to her as a mother her babe.

ELIZABETH GOUDGE
Island Magic 1941

"Christmas won't be Christmas without any presents," grumbled Jo, lying on the rug.

"You know the reason mother proposed not having any presents this Christmas, was because it's going to be a hard winter for everyone; and she thinks we ought not to spend money for pleasure, when our men are suffering so in the army. We can't do much, but we can make our little sacrifices, and ought to do it gladly."

Jo was the first to wake in the gray dawn of Christmas morning. No stockings hung at the fireplace, and for a moment she felt as much disappointed as she did long ago, when her little sock fell down because it was so crammed with goodies. Then she remembered her mother's promise, and slipping her hand under her pillow, drew out a little crimson-covered book. She knew it very well, for it was that beautiful old story of the best life ever lived, and Jo felt that it was a true guide-book for any pilgrim going on a long journey. She woke Meg with a "Merry Christmas," and bade her see what was under her pillow. A green-covered book appeared, with the same picture inside, and a few words written by their mother, which made their one present very precious in their eyes. Presently Beth and Amy woke, to rummage and find their little books also, - one dove-coloured, the other blue; and all sat looking at and talking about them, while the East grew rosy with the coming day.

LOUISA M. ALCOTT
Little Women 1868

Susan awoke in the dark of Christmas morning. A weight lay on her feet, and she moved her toes up and down. She sat up and rubbed her eyes. It was Christmas Day. She stretched out her hands and found the knobby little stocking, which she brought into bed with her and clasped tightly in her arms as she fell asleep again.

She awoke later and lay holding her happiness, enjoying the moment. The light was dim, but the heavy mass of the chest of drawers stood out against the pale walls, all blue like the snowy shadows outside. She drew her curtains and looked out at the starry sky. She listened for the bells of the sleigh, but no sound came through the stillness except the screech owl's call.

She pinched the stocking from the toe to the top, where her white suspender tapes were stitched. It was full of nice knobs and lumps, and a flat thing like a book stuck out of the top. She drew it out – it *was* a book, just what she wanted most.

Next came an apple, with its sweet, sharp odour. She took a bite with her strong, white, little teeth and scrunched it in the dark. There was a tin ball that unscrewed and was filled with comfits, and an orange, and a sugar mouse, all these were easy to feel, a sugar watch with a paper face and a chain of coloured ribbon, a doll's chair and a penny china doll with a round smooth head. She at once named it Diana. She put her next to her skin down the neck of her nightdress, and pulled the last little bumps out of the stocking toe. There were walnuts, and a silver shilling, the only one she ever got, and very great wealth, but it was intended for the money-box in the hall. It was the nicest Christmas stocking she had ever had, and she hugged her knees up to her chin and rocked with joy.

ALISON UTTLEY
The Country Child 1931

William awoke and rubbed his eyes. It was Christmas Day – the day to which he had looked forward with mingled feelings for twelve months. It was a jolly day of course – presents and turkey and crackers and staying up late.

He leapt lightly out of bed and dressed. Then he began to arrange his own gifts to his family. For his father he had bought a bottle of highly-coloured sweets, for his elder brother Robert (aged nineteen) he had expended a vast sum of money on a copy of "The Pirates of the Bloody Hand". These gifts had cost him much thought. The knowledge that his father never touched sweets, and that Robert professed scorn of pirate stories, had led him to hope that the recipients of his gifts would make no objection to the unobtrusive theft of them by their recent donor in the course of the next few days. For his grown-up sister Ethel he had bought a box of coloured chalks. That also might come in useful later. Funds now had been running low, but for his mother he had bought a small cream jug which, after fierce bargaining, the man had let him have at half-price because it was cracked.

Singing "Christians Awake!" at the top of his lusty young voice, he went along the landing, putting his gifts outside the doors of his family, and pausing to yell "Happy Christmas" as he did so. From within he was greeted in each case by muffled groans.

He went downstairs into the hall, still singing. It was earlier than he thought – just five o'clock.

RICHMAL CROMPTON
More William 1922

"She's coming! Strike up, Beth, open the door, Amy. Three cheers for Marmee!" cried Jo, prancing about, while Meg went to conduct mother to the seat of honour.

Beth played her gayest march, Amy threw open the door, and Meg enacted escort with great dignity. Mrs March was both surprised and touched; and smiled with her eyes full as she examined her presents, and read the little notes which accompanied them. The slippers went on at once, a new handkerchief was slipped into her pocket, well scented with Amy's Cologne, the rose was fastened in her bosom, and the nice gloves were pronounced "a perfect fit".

There was a good deal of laughing, and kissing, and explaining, in the simple, loving fashion which makes these home-festivals so pleasant at the time, so sweet to remember long afterwards.

LOUISA M. ALCOTT
Little Women 1868

We had a living room and kitchen and we ran into the kitchen and all the stockings were hanging on the mantelpiece and they would be stuffed three-quarters full with newspaper. We got a beautiful orange, a new penny, a piece of shortbread, and a toffee. Then you went down to play with your pals to see what they got, and nearly everybody got the same thing.

MADGE STRACHAN
Between the wars. (Christmas Past, Gavin Weightman and Steve Humphries)

Christmas was the only time of the year I ever got a new dress. Most of the time it was just jumble sale stuff; shoes were second hand; mum even used to cut up her old flannelette nightdress to make petticoats. I remember when I was eight, mum used to pay sixpence every so often to a dressmaker, and she made me a velvet dress for Christmas. I can see it now with its little lace collar, and it was laid over the back of a chair on Christmas morning. I thought it was marvellous! I wore it Christmas Day and Boxing Day, then it was put away for best – Sunday best – because you didn't want to wear it out too quickly.

LIL HEMMINGS
Between the wars. (Christmas Past, Gavin Weightman and Steve Humphries)

Before the war we didn't celebrate Christmas very much really because we were what was classed as a poor family in those days. We only had a stocking with a few sweets, fruit, and a very small toy. But when I was evacuated it was entirely different, because I went to a middle-aged couple who had no children and they idolised me. I was the "pretty little girl with the black ringlets".

My first Christmas I remember very well. They said, "Go into the front room and there'll be a surprise for you under the armchair." When I looked there was this big white box with this beautiful doll in it. It was a china doll and I don't remember having a doll before that in my life. And we had a Christmas tree and Christmas crackers – things like that which I'd never had at home; I really thought I was in wonderland.

IVY KING
A London evacuee
(Christmas Past, Gavin Weightman and Steve Humphries)

It was the custom for the housekeeper to ask all the servants – perhaps a dozen or more – what they would like for Christmas, then report to the Lady of the house. On Christmas Day they'd all line up and she'd present them with the presents from beneath the tree. The outside staff had a couple of rabbits; perhaps the heads had a pheasant. The presents for the inside staff always took the form of something useful. I still have a strong tin trunk which was such a present way back in 1917.

JACK GOSNEY
(in service) Approx. 1914-18
(Christmas Past, Gavin Weightman and Steve Humphries)

This afternoon a pleasant little festivity has been celebrated at Osborne House, where her Majesty, with an ever-kindly interest in her servants and dependants, has for many years inaugurated Christmas in a similar way, the children of her tenantry and the old and infirm enjoying by the Royal bounty the first taste of Christmas fare.

Until very recently the Queen herself presided at the distribution; but the Princess Beatrice has lately relieved her mother of the fatigue involved; for the ceremony is no mere formality, it is made the occasion of many a kindly word the remembrance of which far outlasts the gifts.

All sorts of rumours are current on the estate for weeks before this Christmas Eve gathering as to the nature of the presents to be bestowed, for no-one is supposed to know beforehand what they will be; but there was a pretty shrewd guess to-day that the boys would be given gloves, and the girls cloaks. In some cases the former had had scarves or cloth for suits, and the latter dresses or shawls. Whatever the Christmas presents may be, here they are, arranged upon tables in two long lines, in the servants' hall. To this holly-decorated apartment the expectant youngsters are brought, and their delighted gaze falls upon a huge Christmas tree laden with beautiful toys. Everybody knows that the tree will be there, and moreover that its summit will be crowned with a splendid doll. Now, the ultimate owner-ship of this doll is a matter of much concern; it needs deliberation, as it is awarded to the best child, and the judges are the children themselves.

The girls are called up first and the steward introduces each child to the Princess Beatrice, to whom he hands the presents that her Royal Highness may bestow them upon the recipients with a word of good will, which makes the day memorable. Then the boys are summoned to participate in the distribution of good things, which consist not only of seasonal and sensible clothing, but toys from the tree, presented by the Queen's grandchildren, who, with their parents, grace the ceremony with their presence and make the occasion one of family interest. Each boy and girl gets in addition a nicely-bound story-book and a large slice of plum pudding neatly packed in paper.

But the hospitality of the Queen is not limited to the children. On al-ternate years the old men and women resident on the estate are given, under the same pleasant auspices, presents of blankets or clothing. To-day it was the turn of the men, and they received tweed for suits. The aged people have their pudding as well. For the farm labourers, who are not bidden to this entertainment, there is a distribution of tickets, each representing a goodly joint of beef for the Christmas dinner.

The festivity this afternoon was brought to a close by the children sing-ing the National Anthem in the courtyard.

A London newspaper
Late 1800 s

Servants are only big children, and are made just as happy as children by little presents and nice things to eat. As great secrecy is observed, the preparations devolve entirely on me, and it is not very easy work, with so many people in our own house and on each of the farms, and all the children, big and little, expecting their share of happiness. The library is uninhabitable for several days before and after, as it is there that we have the trees and presents. All down one side are the trees, and the other three sides are lined with tables, a separate one for each person in the house. When the trees are lighted, and stand in their radiance shining down on the happy faces, I forget all the trouble it has been, and the number of times I have had to run up and down stairs, and the various aches in head and feet, and enjoy myself as much as anybody.

First the June baby is ushered in, then the others and ourselves according to age, then the servants, then come the head inspector and his family, the other inspectors from the different farms, the mamsells, the book-keepers and secretaries, and then all the children, troops and troops of them – the big ones leading the little ones by the hand and carrying the babies in their arms, and the mothers peeping round the door. As many as can get in stand in front of the trees, and sing two or three carols; then they are given their presents, and go off triumphantly.

ELIZABETH VON ARNIM
Elizabeth and her German Garden 1898

"I got this beautiful warm cross-over at the last treat," says old Widow Brown, "and my lady worked it with her own hands, "for," says she, "I've made a bright red border to it, knowing how you like a bit of colour". And the year before I had the loveliest petticoat, and little Missie at The Grange made me a pair of scarlet mittens."

Those who live in villages will be well acquainted with such conversations as this, for they know that the Christmas treat to the poor folk is the great event of the year to them, and one which furnishes the favourite topic of talk and thought for the ensuing twelve months. It is not the amount of money spent on these festivities which makes them so delightful to the humble guests, but the trouble which is taken to ensure a happy evening, and the care with which each individual is provided with a gift which will be just what she wants.

THE LADY
1906

My wife and I used to go overboard at Christmas time on the toys. There'd be so many toys we'd hide them behind the sideboard, and we'd have to move it out from the wall so that there was enough room to put them there. And we had a special Christmas Day ritual. We'd get up early at about six o'clock in the morning and take the presents in and put them round the tree. Then we'd light the fire and put a record on the record player – a Christmas song, Bing Crosby's "White Christmas" was a favourite. Then we'd come out and lock the door and the children were only allowed in when they'd dressed up in their Sunday best, their best trousers and everything, out of respect for Christmas. I think we were sort of compensating for our own childhood when our parents couldn't really afford proper Christmas presents for us, because Christmas now was the highlight of our year. The kids would come up to us and say, "This is the best Christmas we've ever had", and that would make it all worthwhile.

CHARLES McEWAN
1950 s

12

Christmas Morning

It was a convention that the whole family always went to Grandma's on Christmas Day. There would be more than twenty of us, mother and father, aunts and uncles, and not forgetting the maid Esther from the workhouse. You'd always have to wear your Sunday best, suit and shirt and tie and that sort of thing, and you had to be on your best behaviour. It was everyone to Grandma's on Christmas Day, then everybody back to father's – he was the eldest son you see – for Boxing Day.

KEN REED
Early 1900 s
(Christmas Past, Gavin Weightman and Steve Humphries)

As she dressed, memories of other Christmases came unbidden to her mind. Arrival here, at her grandmother's cottage, her eyes eagerly seeking the crib in the hall. She had wanted all the figures in at once – the whole gorgeous impact of it - and had never understood why the Wise Men had to wait until a time when her enthusiasm had waned before they made an appearance.

She remembered, as she put the finishing touches to her hair, how, after they had taken down their stockings and had rushed into their parents' and grandmother's bedrooms to display their treasures and then been told they were to keep quiet while the grown-ups performed all the tedious tasks essential to their toilet, she had tiptoed down the stairs.

The little hall and the rooms leading off it had had the hushed expectancy of spaces on a stage, awaiting the appearance of the actors. At any moment, the door would open and a story would unfold. The sitting-room was the centre, the source of magic. It was so tidy that Florence was overawed. Every vase and carefully placed ornament seemed to glisten like jewels.

Someone had come down very early and lit the fire: the flames flickered and the logs crackled to an unseen audience. On the side tables and on the window-ledges were boxes of dates and peppermint creams, bowls of walnuts and brazil nuts, round wooden boxes of Turkish Delight. Christmas roses formed a garland for a small portrait of the Virgin and Child. A heap of fir cones sprinkled with Jack Frost supported the candles in the centre of the window.

MARY HOCKING
The Very Dead of Winter 1993

On Christmas morning (for the weather was severe) the people made a rough, but brisk and not unpleasant kind of music, in scraping the snow from the pavement in front of their dwellings, and from the tops of their houses, whence it was mad delight to the boys to see it come plumping down into the road below, and splitting into artificial little snow-storms.

The house fronts looked black enough, and the windows blacker, contrasting with the smooth white sheet of snow upon the roofs, and with the dirtier snow upon the ground; which last deposit had been ploughed up in deep furrows by the heavy wheels of carts and waggons. There was nothing very cheerful in the climate or the town, and yet was there an air of cheerfulness abroad that the clearest summer air and brightest summer sun might have endeavoured to diffuse in vain.

For the people who were shovelling away on the house-tops were jovial and full of glee; calling out to one another from the parapets, and now and then exchanging a facetious snowball - better-natured missile far than many a wordy jest - laughing heartily if it went right and not less heartily if it went wrong. The poulterers' shops were still half open, and the fruiterers' were radiant in their glory. There were great, round, pot-bellied baskets of chestnuts, shaped like the waistcoats of jolly old gentlemen, lolling at the doors, and tumbling out into the street in their apoplectic opulence. There were ruddy, brown-faced, broad-girthed Spanish onions, shining in the fatness of their growth like Spanish friars, and winking from their shelves in wanton slyness at the girls as they went by, and glanced demurely at the hung-up mistletoe. There were pears and apples, clustered high in blooming pyramids; there were bunches of grapes, made in the shopkeepers' benevolence to dangle from conspicuous hooks, that people's mouths might water gratis as they passed; there were piles of filberts, mossy and brown, recalling, in their fragrance, ancient walks among the woods, and pleasant shufflings ankle deep through withered leaves; there were Norfolk Biffins, squab and swarthy, setting off the yellow of the oranges and lemons, and, in the great compactness of their juicy persons, urgently entreating and beseeching to be carried home in paper bags and eaten after dinner. The very gold and silver fish, set forth among these choice fruits in a bowl, though members of a dull and stagnant-blooded race, appeared to know that there was something going on; and, to a fish, went gasping round and round their little world in slow and passionless excitement.

The Grocers'! Oh the Grocers'! nearly closed, with perhaps two shutters down, or one; but through those gaps such glimpses! It was not alone that the scales descending on the counter made a merry sound, or that the twine and roller parted company so briskly, or that the cannisters were rattled up and down like juggling tricks, or even that the blended scents of tea and coffee were so grateful to the nose, or even that the raisins were so plentiful and rare, the almonds so extremely white, the sticks of cinnamon so long and straight, the other spices so delicious, the candied fruits so caked and spotted with molten sugar as to make the coldest lookers-on feel faint and subsequently bilious. Nor was it that the figs were moist and pulpy, or that the French plums blushed in modest tartness from their highly-decorated boxes, or that everything was good to eat and in its Christmas dress; but the customers were all so hurried and so eager in the hopeful promise of the day, that they tumbled up against each other at the door, crashing their wicker baskets wildly, and left their purchases upon the counter, and came running back to fetch them, and committed hundreds of the like mistakes, in the best humour possible; while the Grocer and his people were so frank and fresh that the polished hearts with which they fastened their aprons behind might have been their own, worn outside for general inspection, and for Christmas daws to peck at if they chose.

But soon the steeples called good people all, to church and chapel, and away they came, flocking through the streets in their best clothes, and with their gayest faces. And at the same time there emerged from scores of bye-streets, lanes, and nameless turnings, innumerable people, carrying their dinners to the bakers' shops.

CHARLES DICKENS
A Christmas Carol 1843

To our own ivy-covered church we entered at Christmas in a spirit of excitement and wonder, eager to see the beauty, the transformation to a woodland as it seemed to me; and with senses alert and eyes wide we stared at the flowers and berries, we breathed the fragrance of the evergreens, mingled with the scent of the ladies, and the smell of pomatum on the hair of men and boys, and the paraffin in the lamps. We saw branches of scarlet-berried holly on the pulpit and in the long narrow windows which had pictures of the apostles painted on the walls between them. Boughs of yew and trails of ivy were wound round the brass spiral lamp stands and at the ends of each pew. Such a wealth of greenery was there that the woods with their moss and lichens and aromatic leaves seemed to have invaded the church but the beauty lay in the scarlet holly berries brilliantly flashing like lamps.

We knelt on the prickly straw hassocks with tightly shut eyes and then we pressed close to our mother, holding her hand tightly, sniffing the varied odours that filled the church, gazing with intent eyes at the decorations.

The procession of the choir began, and we heard the voices of black-smith, carpenter, wheelwright and bank clerk, men from the Home farm and young boys, who sang with such power and strength they overwhelmed the organ in the church loft: while the congregation also sang lustily, a little behind the choir, and in front of the organ.

So, amid the holly and the ivy, the smell of paraffin, and the scent of the ladies in the squire's pew and the lavender and eau-de-Cologne which lesser people used, we sang our hymns on Christmas Day.

ALISON UTTLEY
Here's a New Day (1956)

Then everybody began to run, last-minute directions about the turkey and the stuffing, hunts for threepenny-bits, for prayer books, for handkerchiefs and lozenges, Tom shouting, "You'll be late again, and Christmas morning", but they got off before the bells began to ring.

Inside it was warm and beautiful, with ivy and holly, and lovely lilies and red leaves from the Court. The rich people wore their silks and furs, all scented and shining. Susan looked at them and wondered about their presents. She had heard they had real Christmas trees, with toys and candles like the one in Hans Andersen, which stood up in a room nearly to the ceiling. She would just like to peep at one for a minute, one minute only, to see if her imagination was right.

She was almost too happy, and her heart ached with joy as she stood on a hassock by her mother's side, with her hymn-book in her hand, singing "Noel, Noel", feasting her eyes on the coloured windows and bright berries and flowers, wrapped in scents and sounds as in a cloud of incense. She buried her face in her muff in ecstasy.

ALISON UTTLEY
The Country Child 1931

Ives was sitting beside Annie in his old neighbourhood church on another Christmas Day looking up at the altar. There were vases with dozens of orchids on either side of the chalice and pots of blossoms set out on the marble floors and against the columns, garlands of ivy strung along the gallery above. In the choir stall they had installed the crèche with its figures of the shepherds and kings and angels on high and the Holy Family inside the stable, the baby Jesus, the light of this world at its centre. And they had covered the roof of the stable with evergreen boughs and someone had burned fragrant incense. That morning as Ives first walked into the sanctuary again, hat in hand and with his wife by his side, he remembered that beautiful and familiar glory.

OSCAR HIJUELOS
Mr Ives' Christmas 1995

The village church, on Christmas Day, was aglow with candles, berried holly, and Christmas roses. The silver on the altar gleamed from Miss Fuller's ministrations, for she would allow no other hand to touch it.

The vicar was in his most festive robes. He gleamed with gold thread and rich embroidery as he mounted the steps to the pulpit and Anna soon found her attention wandering as his light amiable voice fluttered its way to his unusually numerous congregation.

"And now to God the Father" floated from the pulpit, and Anna rose to her feet feeling uncommonly guilty, for not a word of the good vicar's homily had reached her.

But, as she greeted friends outside, she was conscious of a feeling of well-being within her and could only suppose that, by a process akin to osmosis, she had drawn in spiritual grace from her lovely surroundings.

MISS READ
Fresh from the Country 1960

The music on Christmas mornings was frequently below the standard of church-performances at other times. The boys were sleepy from the heavy exertions of the night; the men were slightly wearied; and now, in addition to these constant reasons, there was a dampness in the atmosphere that still further aggravated the evil. Their strings, from the recent long exposure to the night air, rose whole semitones, and snapped with a loud twang at the most silent moment; which necessitated more retiring than ever to the back of the gallery, and made the gallery throats quite husky with the quantity of coughing and hemming required for tuning in.

THOMAS HARDY
Under the Greenwood Tree 1872

While we were talking, we heard the distant toll of the village bell, and I was told that the Squire was a little particular in having his household at church on Christmas morning; considering it a day of pouring out of thanks and rejoicing.

As the morning, though frosty, was remarkably fine and clear, the most of the family walked to the church, which was a very old building of grey stone, and stood near a village, about half a mile from the park gate. Adjoining it was a low snug parsonage, which seemed coeval with the church. The front of it was perfectly matted with a yew tree, that had been trained against its walls; through the dense foliage of which, apertures had been formed to admit light into the small antique lattices. As we passed this sheltered nest, the parson issued forth, and preceded us.

On reaching the church porch, we found the parson rebuking the grey-headed sexton for having used mistletoe among the greens with which the church was decorated. It was, he observed, an unholy plant; profaned by having been used by the Druids in their mystic ceremonies; and though it might be innocently employed in the festive ornamenting of halls and kitchens, yet it had been deemed by the fathers of the church as unhallowed, and totally unfit for sacred purposes. So tenacious was he on this point, that the poor sexton was obliged to strip down a great part of the humble trophies of his taste, before the parson would consent to enter upon the service of the day.

The parson gave us a most erudite sermon on the rites and ceremonies of Christmas, and the propriety of observing it, not merely as a day of thanksgiving, but of rejoicing; supporting the correctness of his opinions by the earliest usages of the church, and enforcing them by the authorities of Theophilus of Caesarea, St. Cyprian, St. Chrysostom, St. Augustine, and a cloud more of saints and fathers, from whom he made copious quotations. I was a little at a loss to perceive the necessity of such a mighty array of forces to maintain a point which no one present seemed inclined to dispute; but I soon found that the good man had a legion of ideal adversaries to contend with, having, in the course of his researches on the subject of Christmas, got completely embroiled in the sectarian controversies of the revolution, when the Puritans made such a fierce assault upon the ceremonies of the church, and poor old Christmas was driven out of the land by proclamation of Parliament. The worthy parson lived but with times past, and knew but little of the present.

I have seldom known a sermon attended apparently with more immediate effects; for on leaving the church the congregation seemed one and all possessed with gayety of spirit so earnestly enjoined by their pastor. The elder folks gathered in knots in the church yard, greeting and shaking hands, and the children ran about shouting Ule! Ule! and repeating some uncouth rhymes, which the parson, who had joined us, informed me had been handed down from days of yore. The villagers doffed their hats to the Squire as he passed, giving him the good wishes of the season with every appearance of heartfelt sincerity, and were invited by him to the hall, to take something to keep out the cold of the weather; and I heard blessings uttered by several of the poor, which convinced me that, in the midst of his enjoyments, the worthy old cavalier had not forgotten the true Christmas virtue of charity.

On our way homeward, his heart seemed overflowing with generous and happy feelings. As we passed over a rising ground which commanded something of a prospect, the sounds of rustic merriment now and then reached our ears; the Squire paused for a few moments, and looked around with an air of inexpressible benignity. "I love," said he, "to see this day well kept by rich and poor; it is a great thing to have one day in the year at least, when you are sure of being welcome wherever you go, and of having, as it were, the world all thrown open to you."

WASHINGTON IRVING
Sketch Book 1820

All over the city men and women and children poured out of the chapels and churches exclaiming at the beauty of the day. It all looked as pretty as a picture, they said. The frost kept the sparkling snow from slipping away from roofs and chimney pots, but it was not too cold to spoil the sunshine. There was no wind. On their way home, whenever a distant view opened out, they could pause and enjoy it without having to shiver. The stretch of the snow-covered fen almost took their breath away, it was so beautiful under the blue arc of the sky. When they turned and looked up at the Cathedral its snow-covered towers seemed to rise to an immeasurable height. Then a wonderful fragrance assailed their nostrils. In steam-filled kitchens the windows had been opened now that the day was warming up. The turkeys and baked potatoes and plum puddings were also warming up and in another forty minutes would have reached the peak of their perfection. Abruptly Christmas Day swung over like a tossed coin. The silver and blue of bells and hymns and angels went down with a bang and was replaced by the red and gold of flaming plum puddings and candled trees. Everyone hurried home as fast as they could.

ELIZABETH GOUDGE
The Dean's Watch 1960

We had not been long home when the sound of music was heard from a distance. A band of country lads without coats, their shirt sleeves fancifully tied with ribands, their hats decorated with greens, and clubs in their hands, were seen advancing up the avenue, followed by a large number of villagers and peasantry. They stopped before the hall door, where the music struck up a peculiar air, and the lads performed a curious and intricate dance, advancing, retreating and striking their clubs together, keeping exact time to the music; while one, whimsically crowned with a fox's skin, the tail of which flaunted down his back, kept capering round the skirts of the dance, and rattling a Christmas box with many antic gesticulations.

After the dance was concluded, the whole party was entertained with brawn and beef, and stout home brewed. The Squire himself mingled among the rustics, and was received with awkward demonstrations of deference and regard. It is true, I perceived two or three of the younger peasants, as they were raising their tankards to their mouths, when the Squire's back was turned, making something of a grimace, and giving each other the wink, but the moment they caught my eye they pulled grave faces, and were exceedingly demure.

The bashfulness of the guests soon gave way before good cheer and affability. There is something genuine and affectionate in the gayety of the lower orders, when it is excited by the bounty and familiarity of those above them; the warm glow of gratitude enters into their mirth, and a kind word, and a small pleasantry frankly uttered by a patron, gladdens the heart of the dependent more than oil and wine. When the Squire had retired, the merriment increased, and there was much joking and laughter; the whole house indeed seemed abandoned to merriment.

WASHINGTON IRVING
Sketch Book 1820

Inside the tiny living-room of the cottage I was ushered to the best chair by the fireside where two rough logs blazed and crackled.

"Bring t'cake out for Mr Herriot, mother," the farmer cried as he rummaged in the pantry. He reappeared with a bottle of whisky at the same time as his wife bustled in carrying a cake thickly laid with icing and ornamented with coloured spangles, toboggans and reindeers.

Mr Kirby unscrewed the stopper. "You know, mother, we're lucky to have such men as this to come out on a Christmas mornin' to help us."

"Aye, we are that." The old lady cut a thick slice of the cake and placed it on a plate by the side of an enormous wedge of Wensleydale cheese . . . .

I took a bite of the cake and followed it with a moist slice of cheese. When I had first come to Yorkshire I had been aghast when offered this unheard-of combination, but time had brought wisdom and I had discovered that the mixture, when chewed boldly together, was exquisite; and, strangely, I had also found that there was nothing more suitable for washing it finally over the tonsils than a draught of raw whisky.

"You don't mind t'wireless, Mr Herriot?" Mrs Kirby asked. "We always like to have it on Christmas morning to hear t'old hymns but I'll turn it off if you like."

"No, please leave it, it sounds grand." I turned to look at the old radio with its chipped wooden veneer, the ornate scroll-work over the worn fabric; it must have been one of the earliest models and it gave off a tinny sound, but the singing of the church choir was none the less sweet . . . ."Hark the Herald Angels Sing" – flooding the little room, mingling with the splutter of the logs and the soft voices of the old people.

JAMES HERRIOT
Let Sleeping Vets Lie 1978

95

13
Christmas Dinner

Christmas is here;
Winds whistle shrill,
Icy and chill.
Little care we;
Little we fear
Weather without,
Sheltered about
The mahogany tree.

W.M. THACKERAY (1811 – 1863)
The Sparkling Bough

So, now is come our joyfulst feast,
    Let every man be jolly;
Each room with ivy leaves is drest,
    And every post with holly.
Though some churls at our mirth repine,
Round your foreheads garlands twine;
Drown sorrow in a cup of wine,
    And let us all be merry.

Now all our neighbours' chimnies smoke,
And Christmas logs are burning;
Their ovens they with bak't meats choke,
And all their spits are turning.
Without the door let sorrow lie;
And if for cold it hap to die,
We'll bury't in a Christmas pye,
And ever more be merry.

Then wherefore in these merry days
Should we, I pray, be duller?
No, let us sing some roundelays
To make our mirth the fuller.
And whilst we thus inspired sing,
Let all the streets with echoes ring;
Woods, and hills, and every thing
Bear witness we are merry.

GEORGE WITHER
Juvenilia 1622

The boar's head, in ancient times, formed the most important dish on the table, and was invariably the first placed on the board upon Christmas Day, being preceded by a body of servitors, a flourish of trumpets, and other marks of distinction and reverence, and carried into the hall by the individual of next rank to the lord of the feast. At some of our colleges and inns of court, the serving of the boar's head on a silver platter on Christmas Day is a custom still followed; and till very lately, a boar's head was competed for at Christmas time by the young men of a rural parish in Essex.

MRS BEETON
Annual 1861

The dinner was served up in the great hall, where the Squire always held his Christmas banquet. A blazing, crackling fire of logs had been heaped on to warm the spacious apartment, and the flame went sparkling and wreathing up the wide-mouthed chimney. The great picture of the crusader and his white horse had been profusely decorated with greens for the occasion, and holly and ivy had likewise been wreathed round the helmet and weapons on the opposite wall, which I understood were the arms of the same warrior. A sideboard was set out just under this chivalric trophy, on which was a display of plate; flagons, cans, cups, beakers, goblets, basins, and ewers; the gorgeous utensils of good companionship, that had gradually accumulated through many generations of jovial housekeepers; before these stood the two Yule candles beaming like two stars of the first magnitude; other lights were distributed in branches, and the whole array glittered like a firmament of silver.

The parson said grace, which was not a short familiar one, such as is commonly addressed to the deity, in these unceremonious days; but a long, courtly, well worded one, of the ancient school. There was now a pause, as if something was expected when suddenly the Butler entered the hall, with some degree of bustle: he was attended by a servant on each side with a large wax light, and bore a silver dish, on which was an enormous pig's head, decorated with rosemary, with a lemon in its mouth, which was placed with great formality at the head of the table. The moment this pageant made its appearance, the harper struck up a flourish; at the conclusion of which the young Oxonian, on receiving a hint from the Squire, gave, with an air of the most comic gravity, an old carol, the first verse of which was as follows:

Caput apri defero
Reddens laudes Domino.
The boar's head in hand bring I,
With garlands gay and rosemary.
I pray you all synge merily
Qui estis in convivio.

The table was literally loaded with good cheer, and presented an epitome of country abundance, in this season of overflowing larders. A distinguished post was allotted to "ancient sirloin," as mine host termed it, being, as he added, "the standard of old English hospitality, and a joint of goodly presence, and full of expectation". There were several dishes quaintly decorated, and which had evidently something traditionary in their embellishments, but about which, as I did not like to appear over curious, I asked no questions.

I could not, however, but notice a pie, magnificently decorated with peacock's feathers, in imitation of the tail of that bird, which overshadowed a considerable tract of the table. This, the Squire confessed with some little hesitation, was a pheasant pie, though a peacock pie was certainly the most authentical; but there had been such a mortality among the peacocks this season, that he could not prevail upon himself to have one killed.

When the cloth was removed, the butler brought in a huge silver vessel of rare and curious workmanship, which he placed before the Squire. Its appearance was hailed with acclamation; being the Wassail Bowl, so renowned in Christmas festivity. The contents had been prepared by the Squire himself; for it was a beverage in the skilful mixture of which he particularly prided himself; alleging that it was too abstruse and complex for the comprehension of an ordinary servant. It was a potation, indeed, that might well make the heart of a toper leap within him; being composed of the richest and raciest wines, highly spiced and sweetened, with roasted apples bobbing about on the surface.

The old gentleman's countenance beamed with a serene look of indwelling delight, as he stirred this mighty bowl. Having raised it to his lips, with a hearty wish for a merry Christmas to all present, he sent it brimming round the board, for every one to follow his example, according to the primitive style; pronouncing it, "the ancient fountain of good feeling, where all hearts met together". There was much laughing and rallying as the honest emblem of Christmas joviality circulated, and was kissed rather coyly by the ladies.

Much of the conversation during dinner turned upon family topics, to which I was a stranger. There was, however, a great deal of rallying of Master Simon about some gay widow, with whom he was accused of having a flirtation,

The dinner time passed away in this flow of innocent hilarity, and though the old hall may have resounded in its time with many a scene of broader rout and revel, yet I doubt whether it ever witnessed more honest and genuine enjoyment.

WASHINGTON IRVING
Sketch Book
1820

You might have thought a goose the rarest of all birds; a feathered phenomenon, to which a black swan was a matter of course; and in truth, it was something like it in that house. Mrs Cratchit made the gravy (ready beforehand in a little saucepan) hissing hot; Master Peter mashed the potatoes with incredible vigour; Miss Belinda sweetened up the apple-sauce; Martha dusted the hot plates; Bob took Tiny Tim beside him in a tiny corner at the table; the two young Cratchits set chairs for everybody, not forgetting themselves, and mounting guard upon their posts, crammed spoons into their mouths, lest they should shriek for goose before their turn came to be helped. At last the dishes were set on, and grace was said. It was succeeded by a breathless pause, as Mrs Cratchit, looking slowly all along the carving-knife, prepared to plunge it in the breast; but when she did, and when the long expected gush of stuffing issued forth, one murmur of delight arose all round the board, and even Tiny Tim, excited by the two young Cratchits, beat on the table with the handle of his knife, and feebly cried Hurrah!

There never was such a goose. Bob said he didn't believe there ever was such a goose cooked. Its tenderness and flavour, size and cheapness, were the themes of universal admiration. Eked out by apple-sauce and mashed potatoes, it was a sufficient dinner for the whole family; indeed, as Mrs Cratchit said with great delight (surveying one small atom of a bone upon the dish), they hadn't ate it all at last! Yet every one had had enough, and the youngest Cratchits in particular were steeped in sage and onion to the eye-brows! But now, the plates being changed by Miss Belinda, Mrs Cratchit left the room alone – too nervous to bear witness – to take the pudding up, and bring it in.

Suppose it should not be done enough! Suppose it should break in turning out! Suppose somebody should have got over the wall of the backyard, and stolen it, while they were merry with the goose - a supposition at which the two young Cratchits became livid! All sorts of horrors were supposed.

Hallo! A great deal of steam! The pudding was out of the copper. A smell like a washing-day! That was the cloth. A smell like an eating-house and a pastry-cook's next door to each other, with a laundress's next door to that! That was the pudding! In half a minute Mrs Cratchit entered, flushed, but smiling proudly, with the pudding like a speckled cannon-ball, so hard and firm, blazing in half of half-a-quartern of ignited brandy, and bedight with Christmas holly stuck into the top.

Oh, a wonderful pudding! Bob Cratchit said, and calmly too, that he regarded it as the greatest success achieved by Mrs Cratchit since their marriage. Mrs Cratchit said that now the weight was off her mind, she would confess she had had her doubts about the quantity of flour. Everybody had something to say about it, but nobody said or thought it was at all a small pudding for so large a family. It would have been flat heresy to do so. Any Cratchit would have blushed to hint at such a thing.

At last the dinner was all done, the cloth was cleared, the hearth swept, and the fire made up. The compound in the jug being tasted, and considered perfect, apples and oranges were put upon the table, and a shovelful of chestnuts on the fire. Then all the Cratchit family drew round the hearth, in what Bob Cratchit called a circle, meaning a half a one; and at Bob Cratchit's elbow stood the family display of glass – two tumblers, and a custard-cup without a handle.

These held the hot stuff from the jug, however, as well as golden goblets would have done; and Bob served it out with beaming looks, while the chestnuts on the fire spluttered and cracked noisily. Then Bob proposed:

"A Merry Christmas to us all, my dears. God bless us!"

Which all the family re-echoed.

"God bless us every one!" said Tiny Tim, the last of all.

CHARLES DICKENS
A Christmas Carol 1843

In the middle of the table was a Christmas tree, alive and growing, looking very much surprised at itself, for had not Tom dug it up from the plantation whilst they were at church, and brought it in with real snow on its branches?

Susan was amazed. If an angel from heaven had sat on the table she would have been less surprised. She ran to hug everybody, her heart was full.

The potatoes were balls of snow, the sprouts green as if they had just come from the garden, as indeed they had, for they too had been dug out of the snow not long before. The turkey was brown and crisp, it had been Susan's enemy for many a day, chasing her from the poultry-yard, and now it was brought low; the stuffing smelled of summer and the herb garden in the heat of the sun.

As for the plum pudding with its spray of red berries and shiny leaves and its hidden sixpence, which would fall out, and land on Susan's plate, it was the best they had ever tasted.

ALISON UTTLEY
The Country Child 1931

Then they all came home to a fine old English early dinner at three o'clock – a sirloin of beef a foot-and-a-half broad, a turkey as big as an ostrich, a plum-pudding bigger than the turkey, and two or three dozen mince-pies. "That's a very large bit of beef," said Mr Jones, who had not lived much in England latterly. "It won't look so large," said the old gentleman, "when all our friends downstairs have had their say to it. A plum-pudding on Christmas Day can't be too big," he said again, "if the cook will but take time enough over it. I never knew a bit go to waste yet."

ANTHONY TROLLOPE
Christmas at Thompson Hall 1876

It was somewhere about my twelfth Christmas, when I and all our family were assembled in the great dining-room of grandpapa. There were three Christmas puddings brought to the table, and they were every one eaten. The puddings were all large, and the Hardys were all well, and ate as the heroes of Homer might be supposed to do. There was not a vestige of the puddings left, and none was intended to be left, though there were four cooked, the servants having a whole one to themselves. This was, on festive occasions, invariably grandpapa's rule.

LETITIA HARDY
Autobiography of a Christmas Pudding
(Mrs Beeton's Christmas Annual 1868)

14
Christmas Afternoon

After the dinner table was removed, the hall was given up to the younger members of the family, who, prompted to all kinds of noisy mirth by the Oxonian and Master Simon, made its old walls ring with their merriment, as they played at romping games.

Whilst we were all attention to the parson's stories, our ears were suddenly assailed by a burst of heterogenous sounds from the hall, in which were mingled something like the clang of rude minstrelsy, with the uproar of many small voices and girlish laughter. The door suddenly flew open, and a train came trooping into the room. That indefatigable spirit, Master Simon, in the faithful discharge of his duties as Lord of Misrule, had conceived the idea of a Christmas mummery, or masqueing; and having called to his assistance the Oxonian and the young officer, who were equally ripe for any thing that should occasion romping and merriment, they had carried it into instant effect. The old housekeeper had been consulted; the antique clothes presses and wardrobes rummaged, and made to yield up the reliques of finery that had not seen the light for several generations; the younger part of the company had been privately convened from parlour and hall, and the whole had been bedizened out, into a burlesque imitation of an antique masque.

Master Simon led the van, as "Ancient Christmas," quaintly apparelled in a ruff, a short cloak, which had very much the aspect of one of the old housekeeper's petticoats, and a hat that might have served for a village steeple. From under this his nose curved boldly forth, flushed with a frost-bitten bloom, that seemed the very trophy of a December blast. He was accompanied by the blue-eyed romp, dished up as "Dame Mince Pie," in the venerable magnificence of faded brocade, long stomacher, peaked hat, and high heeled shoes. The young officer appeared as Robin Hood, in a sporting dress of Kendal green, and a foraging cap with a gold tassel. The costume, to be sure, did not bear testimony to deep research, and there was an evident eye to the picturesque, natural to a young gallant in the presence of his mistress. The fair Julia hung on his arm in a pretty rustic dress, as "Maid Marian". The rest of the train had been metamorphosed in various ways, the girls trussed up in the finery of the ancient belles of the Bracebridge line, and the striplings bewhiskered with burnt cork, and gravely clad in broad skirts, hanging sleeves, and full bottomed wigs, to represent the characters of Roast Beef, Plum Pudding, and other worthies celebrated in ancient masquings.

The irruption of this motley crew, with beat of drum, according to ancient custom, was the consummation of uproar and merriment. Master Simon covered himself with glory by the stateliness with which, as Ancient Christmas, he walked a minuet with the peerless, though giggling, Dame Mince Pie. It was followed by a dance of all the characters, which, from its medley of costumes, seemed as though the old family portraits had skipped down from their frames to join in the sport. Different centuries were figuring at cross hands and right and left; the dark ages were cutting pirouettes and rigadoons; and the days of Queen Bess jigging merrily down the middle, through a line of succeeding generations.

The worthy Squire contemplated these fantastic sports, and this resurrection of his old wardrobe, with the simple relish of childish delight. He stood chuckling and rubbing his hands, and scarcely hearing a word the parson said.

For my part, I was in a continual excitement from the varied scenes of whim and innocent gayety passing before me. It was inspiring to see wild eyed frolick and warm hearted hospitality breaking out from among the chills and glooms of winter, and old age throwing off its apathy, and catching once more the freshness of youthful enjoyment. There was a quaintness too, mingled with all this revelry that gave it a peculiar zest: it was suited to the time and place; and as the old manor house almost reeled with mirth and wassail, it seemed echoing back the joviality of long departed years.

WASHINGTON IRVING
Sketch Book 1820

"Now," said Wardle, after a substantial lunch, when the agreeable items of strong beer and cherry-brandy, had been done ample justice to; "what say you to an hour on the ice? We shall have plenty of time. Do you slide?"

"I used to do so, on the gutters, when I was a boy," replied Mr Pickwick.

"Try it now," said Wardle.

"Oh do please, Mr Pickwick!" cried all the ladies.

"I should be very happy to afford you any amusement," replied Mr Pickwick, "but I haven't done such a thing these thirty years."

"Pooh! Pooh! Nonsense!" said Wardle, dragging off his skates with the impetuosity which characterised all his proceedings. "Here; I'll keep you company; come along!" And away went the good-tempered old fellow down the slide.

Mr Pickwick paused, considered, pulled off his gloves and put them in his hat: took two or three short runs, baulked himself as often, and at last took another run, and went slowly and gravely down the slide, with his feet about a yard and a quarter apart, amidst the gratified shouts of all the spectators.

"Keep the pot a bilin', sir!" said Sam; and down went Wardle again, and then Mr Pickwick, and then Sam, and then Mr Winkle, and then Mr Bob Sawyer, and then the fat boy, and then Mr Snodgrass, following closely upon each other's heels, and running after each other with as much eagerness as if all their future prospects in life depended on their expedition.

It was the most intensely interesting thing, to observe the manner in which Mr Pickwick performed his share in the ceremony; to watch the torture of anxiety with which he viewed the person behind, gaining upon him at the imminent hazard of tripping him up; to see him gradually expend the painful force he had put on at first, and turn slowly round on the slide, with his face towards the point from which he had started; to contemplate the playful smile which mantled on his face when he had accomplished the distance, and the eagerness with which he turned round when he had done so, and ran after his predecessor: his black gaiters tripping pleasantly through the snow, and his eyes beaming cheerfulness and gladness through his spectacles. And when he was knocked down (which happened upon the average every third round), it was the most invigorating sight that can possibly be imagined, to behold him gather up his hat, gloves, and handkerchief, with a glowing countenance, and resume his station in the rank, with an ardour and enthusiasm that nothing could abate.

The sport was at its height, the sliding was at the quickest, the laughter was at the loudest, when a sharp smart crack was heard. There was a quick rush towards the bank, a wild scream from the ladies, and a shout from Mr Tupman. A large mass of ice disappeared; the water bubbled up over it; Mr Pickwick's hat, gloves, and handkerchief were floating on the surface; and this was all of Mr Pickwick that anybody could see.

Dismay and anguish were depicted on every countenance, the males turned pale, and the females fainted, Mr Snodgrass and Mr Winkle grasped each other by the hand, and gazed at the spot where their leader had gone down, with frenzied eagerness: while Mr Tupman, by way of rendering the promptest assistance, and at the same time conveying to any persons who might be within hearing, the clearest possible notion of the catastrophe, ran off across the country at his utmost speed, screaming "Fire!" with all his might.

It was at this moment, when old Wardle and Sam Weller were approaching the hole with cautious steps, that a face, head, and shoulders, emerged from beneath the water, and disclosed the features and spectacles of Mr Pickwick.

"Keep yourself up for an instant – for only one instant!" bawled Mr Snodgrass.

"Yes, do; let me implore you – for my sake!" roared Mr Winkle, deeply affected. The adjuration was rather unnecessary; the probability being, that if Mr Pickwick had declined to keep himself up for anybody else's sake, it would have occurred to him that he might as well do so, for his own.

"Do you feel the bottom there, old fellow?" said Wardle.

"Yes, certainly," replied Mr Pickwick, wringing the water from his head and face, and gasping for breath. "I fell upon my back. I couldn't get on my feet at first."

The clay upon so much of Mr Pickwick's coat as was yet visible, bore testimony to the accuracy of this statement; and as the fears of the spectators were still further relieved by the fat boy's suddenly recollecting that the water was nowhere more than five feet deep, prodigies of valour were performed to get him out. After a vast quantity of splashing, and cracking, and struggling, Mr Pickwick was at length fairly extricated from his unpleasant position, and once more stood on dry land.

"Oh, he'll catch his death of cold," said Emily.

"Dear old thing!" said Arabella. "Let me wrap this shawl round you, Mr Pickwick."

"Ah, that's the best thing you can do," said Wardle; "and when you've got it on, run home as fast as your legs can carry you, and jump into bed directly."

A dozen shawls were offered on the instant. Three or four of the thickest having been selected, Mr Pickwick was wrapped up, and started off, under the guidance of Mr Weller: presenting the singular phenomenon of an elderly gentleman, dripping wet, and without a hat, with his arms bound down to his sides, skimming over the ground, without any clearly defined purpose, at the rate of six good English miles an hour. But Mr Pickwick cared not for appearances in such an extreme case, and urged on by Sam Weller, he kept at the very top of his speed until he reached the door of Manor Farm. He paused not an instant until he was snug in bed.

Sam Weller lighted a blazing fire in the room, and took up his dinner; a bowl of punch was carried up afterwards, and a grand carouse held in honour of his safety. A second and a third bowl were ordered in; and when Mr Pickwick awoke next morning, there was not a symptom of rheumatism about him: which proves, as Mr Bob Sawyer very justly observed, that there is nothing like hot punch in such cases: and that if ever hot punch did fail to act as a preventive, it was merely because the patient fell into the vulgar error of not taking enough of it.

CHARLES DICKENS
The Pickwick Papers 1837

About half past four on Christmas Day, all the family would go trooping off to Auntie Queenie's. Her house would be packed; all our relatives would be there – the same faces year after year. We'd have ham sandwiches, celery, cheese, and crisps – they were a real treat for us at the time. The living room was so small that only a couple of people could go in and get food at the same time, so we ate in shifts. Then, as the evening wore on, the beer started flowing, the women started to drink sherry, and there'd be fizzy lemonade and dandelion and burdock for the kids.

JIM HUMPHRIES
1920 s
(Christmas Past, Gavin Weightman and Steve Humphries)

15
Christmas Evening

By this time it was getting dark, and snowing pretty heavily; and as Scrooge and the Spirit went along the streets, the brightness of the roaring fires in kitchens, parlours, and all sorts of rooms, was wonderful. Here, the flickering of the blaze showed preparations for a cosy dinner, with hot plates baking through and through before the fire, and deep red curtains, ready to be drawn to shut out cold and darkness. There all the children of the house were running out into the snow to meet their married sisters, brothers, cousins, uncles, aunts, and be the first to greet them. Here, again, were shadows on the window-blind of guests assembling; and there a group of handsome girls, all hooded and fur-booted, and all chattering at once, tripped lightly off to some near neighbour's house; where, woe upon the single man who saw them enter – artful witches, well they knew it – in a glow!

But if you had judged from the numbers of people on their way to friendly gatherings, you might have thought that no one was at home to give them welcome when they got there, instead of every house expecting company, and piling up its fires half-chimney high. The very lamp-lighter, who ran on before, dotting the dusky streets with specks of light, was dressed to spend the evening somewhere.

CHARLES DICKENS
A Christmas Carol 1843

The morning charities and ceremonies took so much time, that the rest of the day was devoted to preparations for the evening festivities. Being still too young to go often to the theatre, and not rich enough to afford any great outlay for private performances, the girls put their wits to work, and, necessity being the mother of invention, made whatever they needed. Very clever were some of their productions; paste-board guitars, antique lamps made of old fashioned butter-boats, covered with silver paper, gorgeous robes of old cotton, glittering with tin spangles from a pickle factory, and armour covered with the same useful diamond-shaped bits, left in sheets when the lids of tin preserve-pots were cut out. The furniture was used to being turned topsy-turvy, and the big chamber was the scene of many innocent revels.

No gentlemen were admitted; so Jo played male parts to her heart's content and took immense satisfaction in a pair of russet-leather boots given her by a friend, who knew a lady who knew an actor. These boots, an old foil, and a slashed doublet once used by an artist for some picture, were Jo's chief treasures, and appeared on all occasions. The smallness of the company made it necessary for the two principal actors to take several parts apiece; and they certainly deserved some credit for the hard work they did in learning three or four parts, whisking in and out of various costumes, and managing the stage besides.

On Christmas night, a dozen girls piled on to the bed, which was the dress circle, and sat before the blue and yellow chintz curtains, in a most flattering state of expectancy. There was a good deal of rustling and whispering behind the curtain, a trifle of lamp-smoke, and an occasional giggle from Amy, who was apt to get hysterical in the excitement of the moment. Presently a bell sounded, the curtains flew apart, and the Operatic Tragedy began.

LOUISA M. ALCOTT
Little Women 1868

Then I went to bed. Looking through my bedroom window, out into the moonlight and the unending smoke-coloured snow, I could see the lights in the windows of all the other houses on our hill and hear the music rising from them up the long, steadily falling night. I turned the gas down, and got into bed. I said some words to the close and holy darkness, and then I fell asleep.

DYLAN THOMAS
A Child's Christmas in Wales (Published posthumously 1955)

Through the blue dusk of a perfect Christmas Day the guests drove to the Herb of Grace. The gate had been left open for them, and the oak trees seemed to bend over them in a friendly sort of way as they bumped their way along the lane. The sky was cloudless, and the few stars that had appeared shone very brightly, giving promise of a blaze of glory to come. At the turn of the lane they heard the owl hooting in Knyghtwood, but the ghostly trees upon either side made no sound, for it was a windless night. The lanterns had been lit and placed upon the walls, and down at the bottom of the lane they could see the glint of them upon the water. Lights streamed from the Herb of Grace, from every window and from the open front door, and the very jubilation of that light had something to say of the utter happiness of the day that had been spent within.

As they were divested of their wraps they exclaimed in delight at the appearance of the wide old hall, with the yule log blazing on the hearth and the holly-wreathed lights burning in their candle-sconces all around the walls. Their seats had been arranged diagonally across the hall to face the L-shaped stage. At its angle stood the glorious Christmas tree, bright with lighted candles. In the end, as it represented Knyghtwood, it had been decided to give it no decoration except the candles that burned in the wood at sunset. And it needed no other, for the candles shone so gloriously.

The guests became conscious of a delightful jovial glow of hospitable warmth wrapping them round.

ELIZABETH GOUDGE
The Herb of Grace 1948

Midnight strikes. You hear it in the silence of Christmas night as you hear it at no other time of the year. The great day has come to an end.

A London newspaper
Late 1800 s

16
Looking Back

When the time came it was for all of them – the grown-ups as well as the children – a day of sheer delight, one of those magical times that are not forgotten while life lasts, when it seems as if nothing can go wrong; as though human imperfection were aided and sustained by something outside itself, and just for once allowed to bring to perfection everything that it attempted.

ELIZABETH GOUDGE
The Herb of Grace 1948

Lay pretty long in bed, and then rose, leaving my wife desirous to sleep, having sat up till four this morning seeing her mayds make mince-pies. I went to church, then home, and dined well on some good ribbs of beef roasted and mince-pies, and plenty of good wine of my owne, and my heart full of true joy and thanks to God Almighty for the goodness of my condition at this day.

SAMUEL PEPYS
Diary, Christmas Day 1666

On Christmas morning we started off the same as any other morning. I got up about quarter past six and got busy with the lamps and cleaned the boots of the family and any visitors there were.

It was my job to see to the fires, clear the dinner table and see the silver safely stored away. Then I'd wash up and place the candles ready for bed and that was the Christmas come and gone.

JACK GOSNEY
(in service) Approx. 1914-1918
(Christmas Past, Gavin Weightman and Steve Humphries)

17
Looking Forward

There was always the Feast of Lights. Our forefathers, we believe, had stouter hearts than we have. But they did fear the eeriness of mid-winter darkness. And so they lit great bonfires on the hills at night to encourage the Sun God. They could not live without the Light of the World. They reached out to him and received the reassurance they longed for.

And so Christmas is still the Feast of Lights. So many of them. Once it was the yule-log, the burning brandy of the snap-dragon game and the flames round the Christmas pudding. Then it was twinkling wax candles on the Christmas tree. Now the candles are mostly electric and the blazing lights in Regent Street are rather garish. But it does not matter, for whatever they are, they continue to be reflections from the Light that at the beginning of all things moved upon the face of the waters, that in the fullness of the days was born to be the glory of Israel and a light to lighten the Gentiles, that in the ending of the days will shine out upon whatever chaos we have brought upon ourselves. "Thou shalt light me a candle," said the psalmist. "Thou shalt turn my darkness into light."

ELIZABETH GOUDGE
Preface, The Christmas Book 1967

Christmas comes but once a year – which is unhappily true, for when it begins to stay with us the whole year round we shall make this earth a very different place.

CHARLES DICKENS
The Seven Poor Travellers 1855

The spirit of Christmas
Is one of good cheer,
Towards all our friends
And those we hold dear.
Oh, let it continue
Throughout the New Year.

Index